The Family and Social Life
of the Puritans

The Family *and* Social Life *of the* Puritans

E Z R A   H O Y T   B Y I N G T O N

THE
Greater Heritage
Christian Publishing
WINTER SPRINGS, FL

The Family and Social Life of the Puritans by Ezra Hoyt Byington
Abridged from *The Puritan in England and New England* (1896) by
Ezra Hoyt Byington
This edition first published February 2023
© 2023 The Greater Heritage

Published by The Greater Heritage
1170 Tree Swallow Dr., Suite 309
Winter Springs, FL 32708
www.thegreaterheritage.com
info@thegreaterheritage.com

All scripture references are taken from the
King James Version (KJV) of the Bible.

Cover Design: The Greater Heritage
Cover Image: *Familie aan de bijbelstudie* (1855) by Auguste Adrien Jouanin, after
Edouard Dubufe. The Rijksmuseum, Museumstraat 1, 1071 XX Amsterdam,
Netherlands. Gift of J.W.E. vom Rath, Amsterdam. RP-P-1917-272.
http://hdl.handle.net/10934/RM0001.COLLECT.130180.
Font(s): Capitolium2, Constantia, Crimson Text, Goodchild Pro,
Kings Caslon, Kings Caslon Display, Vollkorn.

Printed in the United States of America

Library of Congress Control Number: 2022923398

ISBN (hardcover): 978-1-953855-98-5
ISBN (paperback): 978-1-953855-48-0
ISBN (PDF): 978-1-953855-47-3
ISBN (EPUB): 978-1-953855-38-1

1 2 3 4 5 6 7 8 9 10   27 26 25 24 23

No other section of the Anglo-Saxon race has excelled the Puritans in the number of great men and of good men, — soldiers and statesmen and scholars, that it has produced.

PUBLISHER'S NOTE

•

This book is an abridgment of Byington's 1896 work *The Puritan in England and New England*. This non-facsimile version is faithful to its original publication, however slight changes have been made to breathe new life into the title and make it easier to read for contemporary audiences. First, Byington's original sources have been painstakingly researched and updated to help readers and scholars track down original source material for further research. Second, in certain areas spelling and formatting have been updated for easier reading. Lastly, chapter titles have been changed at times and sub-headings added to further help the reader and organize the book according to modern publishing standards. In all other areas original formatting and style have been retained.

CONTENTS

•

A TIMELINE OF PURITAN HISTORY

•

1330 John Wycliffe born.

1382 Wycliffe's New Testament.

1526 Tyndale's New Testament.

1534 Henry VIII acknowledged as "Supreme Head of the Church of England" via the Act of Supremacy.

1535 Coverdale's Bible.

1547 Edward VI ascends the throne.

1553 Mary I becomes Queen.

1555 Persecution of Protestants begins.

1558 Elizabeth I becomes Queen.

Acts of Supremacy and Uniformity.

1564 The name "Puritan" first used.

1565 The Dean of Christ Church, Oxford, imprisoned for Non-conformity.

1572 Massacre of St. Bartholomew's Day.

1576 John Robinson born.

1580 Separatist Church in Norwich under Robert Browne.

1583   Whitgift, Archbishop of Canterbury.

         Ecclesiastical Commission receives new powers.

         Two Puritans hung for Non-conformity.

1588   Defeat of the Spanish Armada.

1588-89 Martin Marprelate tracts.

1593   Barrowe, Greenwood, and Penry publicly executed for their Non-conformity.

1602   The Separatist Church at Gainsborough.

1603   Death of Queen Elizabeth I.

         James I ascends the throne.

         Millenary Petition.

1604   Hampton Court Conference.

1605   Three hundred Ministers expelled from their parishes for Non-conformity.

1606   Church formed at Scrooby.

1607-08 The Pilgrims removed to Amsterdam.

1609   The Pilgrims settled at Leyden.

1611   Authorized Version of the Bible.

1618   Thirty Years' War begun.

1620   The Pilgrims land at Plymouth.

1621   Death of Governor Carver.

         Bradford chosen Governor.

1625   Charles I ascends the throne.

1628   Endicott lands at Salem, with a colony.

1629   A charter granted for the Massachusetts Bay Company.

Agreement to settle in Massachusetts signed, in Cambridge, by Winthrop and others.

Re-enforcements sent to Salem, with Higginson.

Puritan Church formed at Salem, August 6.

1630   Governor Winthrop arrives in Massachusetts with a large colony of Puritans.

Boston settled.

First General Court in Massachusetts.

1633   Laud, Archbishop of Canterbury.

1635   First Settlement in Connecticut.

1636   Harvard College founded.

1637   The first Massachusetts Synod.

The case of John Hampden tried, in England.

1639   The Constitution of Connecticut (Fundamental Orders) adopted.

1640   The Long Parliament met.

The Bay Psalm Book, printed.

1643-49 Westminster Assembly.

New England Confederation.

1644   Death of Elder Brewster.

1646-48 Cambridge Synod (Platform of Church Government)

1649   Execution of Charles I.

1651-52 Hugh Parsons tried in Springfield for Witchcraft.

1653   Oliver Cromwell, Lord Protector.

1656-62 Persecution of the Quakers.

1658   Death of Cromwell.

The Savoy Synod adopts a Confession of Faith.

1660   The Restoration of the Stuarts.

1662   The Boston Synod adopts the Half-Way Covenant.

1673   The first Church organized in Maine, at York.

The Act of Uniformity re-enacted in England.

1679   The Reforming Synod.

1680   The Synod adopts the Savoy Confession.

1691-2   Witchcraft in Salem and elsewhere.

1691   Charter of the Province of Massachusetts.

1701   Yale College founded.

1708   The Saybrook Platform adopted.

1709   The General Association of Connecticut Ministers organized.

1716   Yale College located at New Haven.

1720-50   The Great Awakening.

1727   Jonathan Edwards ordained, Northampton.

1738   The Methodists appear in London.

1740   Whitefield preaches in New England.

1750   Jonathan Edwards dismissed from Northampton.

1754   Edwards' Work on The Freedom of the Will.

1758   Death of President Edwards.

1762   Church in Bennington, Vt., organized.

1769   Dartmouth College founded.

PART I - DAILY LIFE

•

1

ILLUSTRATIONS OF PURITAN LIFE (COL. JOHN HUTCHINSON AND JOHN MILTON)

•

HOME, as we conceive it now," says Mr. John Richard Green, "was the creation of the Puritan." He gives the reason for his statement. "Wife and child rose from mere dependents on the will of husband or father, as husband and father saw in them saints like himself, souls hallowed by the touch of a divine Spirit, and called with a divine calling like his own. The sense of spiritual fellowship gave a new tenderness and refinement to the common family affections."[1]

The philosophic historian is undoubtedly correct. The Puritan had broken away from the old traditions, and from ecclesiastical bonds, and had come into a realm of comparatively free and liberal thought. His fellowship was with the Father, and with His Son, Jesus Christ, without the intervention of the priest or of the Church. So far forth he was a free man, in personal relations with God. All the members of his family were equally free, and equally the favorites of God. This intense individualism opened a new social life, with a broader charity, and a warmer and more absorbing love. It developed a new type of citizenship and has tended undoubtedly toward Democracy. It has

---

1 John Richard Green, *History of the English People Volume 3* (New York: Harper & Brothers, 1879), 19.

lifted the common man to an equality with those in the privileged classes. The religious sentiment of the Puritans has developed the altruistic feeling, so abundant in modern life.

Some illustrations from Puritan history will make these statements plain, and will set forth the reasons for them. We need to know what sort of men and women the Puritans were in their homes.

Mrs. Hutchinson, writing to her children concerning their father, has given a vivid description of that model Puritan, Colonel John Hutchinson, of Owthorpe, who lived in the time of Oliver Cromwell. She says,

He was of a middle stature, of a slender and exactly well-proportional shape in all parts, his hair of light brown, very thick set in his youth, softer than the finest silk, and curling into loose great rings at the ends: his eyes of a lively gray, his visage thin, his mouth well made, and his lips very ruddy and graceful; his teeth even and white as the purest ivory, his forehead not very high, his nose raised and sharp; but withal he had a most amiable countenance, which carried in it something of magnanimity and majesty mixed with sweetness, that at the same time bespoke love and awe in all that saw him.

He was nimble and active and graceful in all his motions; he was apt for any bodily exercise; he could dance admirably well, but neither in youth nor riper years made any practice of it; he had skill in fencing, such as became a gentleman; he had a great love of music; . . . he had good judgment in paintings, graving, sculpture, and all liberal arts, and had many curiosities of all kinds; he took much pleasure in the improvement of grounds, in planting groves and walks, and fruit trees; he was wonderfully neat, cleanly and genteel in his habit.

He hated persecution for religion, and was always a champion for all religious people against all oppressors. Neither in youth, nor riper age could the most fair or enticing women ever draw him into unnecessary familiarity or vain converse or dalliance with them, yet he despised nothing of the female sex but their follies and vanities; wise and virtuous women he loved, and delighted in all pure, holy and unblameable conversation with them. For conjugal affection to his wife, it was such as whosoever would draw out a rule of honor, kindness and religion, need no more, but exactly draw out his example; never man had a greater passion for a woman, nor a more honorable esteem for a wife. He governed by persuasion, which he never employed but to things honorable and profitable for herself; he loved her soul and her honor more than her outside, and yet he had for her person a constant indulgence. So constant was he in his love that when she ceased to be young and lovely, he began to show most fondness; he loved her at such a kind and generous rate as words cannot express. He was as kind a father, as dear a brother, as good a master, and as faithful a friend as the world had.

He understood well, and as well performed when he undertook it, the military art in all parts of it; he naturally loved the employment as it suited with his active temper more than any, conceiving a mutual delight in leading those men that loved his conduct, and when he commanded soldiers, never was man more loved and reverenced by all that were under him, and they joyed as much in his commands as he in their obedience. He had a sweet and loving courtesy to the poorest, and would often employ many spare hours with the commonest soldiers and poorest laborers.[2]

Yet this man, so gentle, so affectionate, so highly cultured, was a Puritan soldier — a Colonel in the army of Cromwell — who fought vigorously through the civil war. He was one of the judges who condemned the king to death. After Oliver Cromwell became Lord Protector, Colonel Hutchinson disclosed to him a plot against his life; and when Cromwell called him "My dear Colonel," and invited him to "come in and take a part" in his government, Hutchinson refused, telling him plainly that he liked not any of his ways since he broke up the Parliament. After the restoration of Charles the Second, Colonel Hutchinson suffered a long and cruel imprisonment, and finally died in prison, because he would not in any way compromise his principles, or betray his friends. This man was one of the Ironsides, and yet his family and social life was as full of sweetness, and tenderness, — of the love of all beautiful and gracious things, — as the lives of those who are the choicest spirits of our own time.

Nor did Hutchinson stand alone among the Puritans of his time. John Milton is the completest type of Puritanism. "His youth shows us," says a recent writer, "how much of the gayety, the poetic ease, the intellectual culture of the Renaissance lingered in a Puritan home." His tract on education is one of the broadest and most liberal treatises of the seventeenth century, — a prophecy of the nineteenth. "Whenever the element of beauty is found in Milton," says Professor Shedd, "it is found in absolute purity. A more absolute beauty and a more

---

2 Lucy Hutchinson, *Memoirs of the Life of Colonel Hutchinson* (London: Henry Bohn, 1863), 22-32.

delicate aerial grace are not to be found than appear in the *Comus*, and the fourth book of *Paradise Lost*."[3]

We read in the records of that age, of a certain Puritan mother, in humble life in England, that "she was very loving and obedient to her parents, loving and true to her husband, very tender-hearted to her children, loving all that were Godly." These illustrations of the Puritan spirit and temper can be multiplied from the records of that age.

---

3 William Greenough Thayer Shedd, *Literary Essays* (New York: Charles Scribner's Sons, 1878), 23.

2

LETTERS OF GOVERNOR WINTHROP
AND HIS WIFE

•

ONE of the reliable sources of information in respect to family and social life is the correspondence between members of families. Such letters are apt to be destroyed, especially the most significant and domestic letters. We have, fortunately, a large number of the letters which passed between Governor John Winthrop and his wife, and also his letters to his son. Winthrop was in many ways the best representative of the early New England Puritans. There is a statue, in one of the public squares of Boston, to John Winthrop, "Founder of Massachusetts," with the Bible in one hand, and the charter of the Colony in the other. Another statue of him is in the chapel of the cemetery at Mount Auburn. Another statue of him, as a representative of the State, stands in the Capitol at Washington. He was for eleven years the Governor of the Colony, and as long as he lived, he was its foremost citizen. From his letters and his journals, we derive our most definite knowledge of the life in the Colony in the first generation. He was born in England, in 1588, so that he was forty-two when he came to New England. Margaret Tyndal was his third wife. When Adam Winthrop, the aged father of John Winthrop, learned that she was betrothed to his son, he sent her a present, with a letter in which he addressed her as "Gentle Mistress Margaret," and assured her of his fatherly love and affection, spelling "Love" with a capital letter, and told her with the frankness of a patriarch, that he thought himself happy that in his old age "I shall enjoy the familiar company of so virtuous and loving a daughter and pass the residue of my days in peace and quietness. I do here faithfully promise for my son that he will always be a most kind and loving husband unto you."

Our first letter from John Winthrop is addressed to "My dearest friend and most heartily beloved Mrs. Marg^t Tyndall." This was before their marriage. The next is addressed to "My only beloved spouse, my most sweet friend, and faithful companion of my pilgrimage, the happy, and hopeful supply (next Christ Jesus) of my greatest losses." He says at the end, "My father and mother salute thee heartily."

The next is addressed to "My dear wife," and was written when she was away from home attending at her mother's bedside in her last sickness. Later, he writes to her as "My Truly Beloved and Dear wife;" "My sweet wife;" "My most Dear and Sweet Spouse;" "My Good Wife;" "My Dear Wife, my Chief Love in this World;" and he subscribes the letters, "Thine;" "Thy faithful husband;" "Thine as his own;" "Thy faithful husband, still present with thee in his most unkind absence;" "So I kiss my sweet wife, and rest, Thy frail but faithful husband."

She begins her letter, "My Dear Husband;" and ends it with, "Your loving and obedient wife;" "Most Dear and Loving Husband," and "Your obedient wife always;" "My most Kind and Loving Husband," "Your loving and obedient wife." In one letter she goes quite beyond all modern precedents, and writes, "Thy unworthy wife."

Here is a letter, written at Groton, in Suffolk, in 1630, (N. S.) addressed to John Winthrop, Esq. at Mr. Downing's house, in Fleet Street, and written just before his departure for New England.

My Dear Husband, — I know thou art desirous to hear often from us, which makes me take pleasure in writing to thee, and in relating my true affections to thee and desires of your wished welfare....I must part with my most dear husband, which is a very hard trial for me to undergo. If the Lord does not support and help me in it, I shall be unable to bear it. I have now received thy kind letter which I cannot read without shedding a great many tears, but I will resign thee, and give thee into the hands of the almighty God, who is all sufficient for thee, whom I trust will keep thee, and prosper thee in the way thou art to go....I know I shall have thy prayers to God for me that what is wanting in thy presence may be supplied by the comfort of God's spirit. I am now full of passion, having newly received thy letter, and not able to write much. My son F. will write about other business. I begin to fear I shall see thee no more before thou goest (to New England) which I should be very sorry for and earnestly intreat thee that thou wilt come once more down if it be possible.

The Governor did "come once more down," after such a letter as that. He wrote:

I purpose (if God will) to be with thee upon Thursday come sunlight, and then I must take my Farewell of thee, for a summers day, and a winters day. The Lord of good God will, (I hope) send us a happy meeting again in his good time: Amen. Among other things let the brassen quart in the Larder house be put up: and my gray cloak and the coat which was my brother Fones: and let this warrant enclosed to sent to Colchester to Mr. Sam Borrowes by the next time the cart goes. The Lord bless thee my sweet wife, with all our children.

Thy faithful husband,
Feb. 5, 1629 - (O. S.) Jo: Winthrop.

Remember to put me up some Cardons and Cardns seed. The reading of (thy letter) has dissolved my head into tears....If I live, I *will see thee ere I go*, I shall part from thee with sorrow enough: be comfortable my most sweet wife.

She wrote again: "I am glad to hear you will come home this week, for I desire to enjoy thy sweet presence as often as I can, before that long parting come which I desire the Lord to fit us for." He writes, February 14th, "Thou must be my valentine, for none hath challenged me." March 2nd, the Governor writes again, having in the meantime been home to Groton to say farewell, and returned to London to complete his arrangements for the voyage to New England. He tells her that their two sons, and most of the servants have already gone to South Hampton: and adds, "Ah my most kind and dear wife, how sweet is thy love to me. The Lord bless thee and thine, with the blessings from above....So I kiss and embrace thee and rest thine ever." March 10th, he wrote again, sending his love to his children by name, including "the little one unknown," and to each of the servants, and to his old neighbors. Four days later, he writes again from Southampton; on the 22nd, there is another letter to his wife, written "aboard the Arabella riding at the Cowes." He writes once more, March 28th, still on board the ship, which had been detained by adverse winds. "Our boys," he says, "are well, and cheerful, and have no mind of home. They lie both with me, and sleep as soundly in a rug, (for we use no sheets here,) as ever they did at Groton: and so do I myself. Mondays and Fridays, at five of the clock at night we shall meet in spirit till we meet in person. Yet if all these hopes should fail, blessed be our God, that we are assured we shall meet one day, if not as husband and wife, yet in a better condition." Once more, before the fleet set out on its voyage, he wrote, April 3rd, to acknowledge two letters from his wife, and to tell her that "on Friday when five of the clock came," he "had respite from his cares" to remember her, and to "parley" with, and meet her "in Spirit before the Lord."

These extracts from this correspondence — two hundred and sixty years old — may give some impression of its quality. Time blots out almost all things written by the hand of man; but there are almost a hundred of these letters, which have been rescued from oblivion, and they give us, almost at first hand, repeated glimpses of the actual life of this representative Puritan family. The correspondence which passed between Governor Winthrop and his son John, cannot be quoted here, for lack of space, but it is, in its own way, as suggestive of the tenderness, and singular wisdom, and piety of this old family, as the correspondence from which these scattered specimen leaves have been selected.[1]

It was the 16th of July before Governor Winthrop had an opportunity to send his next letter. The mails did not cross the Atlantic as frequently then as now. They had a long and tempestuous voyage, and his letter is full of gratitude for their preservation, as well as of affection for those left in the old home at Groton.

It was the 3rd of November (O. S.) of the next year when Mrs.

---

[1] Twenty-seven of these letters were printed in 1825, in the appendix to the first volume of Governor Winthrop's Journal. The others were printed in *The Life and Letters of John Winthrop*, by Hon. Robert C. Winthrop, Boston, 1869, and also in the *Collections of the Massachusetts Historical Society*. Rev. Joseph H. Twichell, of Hartford, Conn., edited an edition of fifty-eight of the letters, with the title, "Some Old Puritan Love Letters," New York, 1893. In this edition the old spelling is very carefully restored.

Winthrop was able to join her husband. She went in the ship Lyon, with his eldest son, and other of his children. Great was the rejoicing at their arrival. "Divers of the Assistants, and most of the people of the near plantations came to welcome them, and brought, and sent, for divers days, great store of provisions, as fat hogs, kids, venison, poultry, geese, partridges, etc., so as the like joy, and manifestation of love had never been seen in New England. It was a great marvel," said Governor Winthrop, "that so much people, and such store of provisions could be gathered together at so few hours warning."[2]

---

2 John Winthrop and James Savage, *The History of New England from 1630 to 1649 Volume I* (Boston: Phelps and Farnham, 1825), 67.

3

SEVENTEENTH CENTURY LIFE

•

IT is not difficult to conjecture what the social and family life would
be in a community made up of such men and women as those seventeenth century Puritans of whom we have been reading. Such
gentleness, and affection, and refinement of feeling, and such piety
would bear fruit in the most beautiful lives.

But the records that have come down to us from the Colonial
period of New England history give us a distinct picture of life as
it actually went on from year to year. It is marvelous how abundant
these records are. Those old Pilgrims had a respect for their mission,
and they were sure that those who should come after them would
desire to know their history.

We have, first of all, the incomparable histories written by Governor Bradford of Plymouth, and by Governor Winthrop of Boston.
They cover the time from the earliest settlements to 1646. We have
also the official records, not only of these two oldest colonies, but
of Rhode Island, Connecticut, and New Hampshire. These are
supplemented by a great number of histories, and narratives, journals,
pamphlets, and treatises, letters and replies, which make the life of

that time luminous to those who will go to the original sources.

What then was the life in the Colonial period of our history? In the first place, it was a life in the earlier part of the seventeenth century. The fathers of New England were very much in advance of their time, and yet they were influenced by the spirit of their times. It is not only unwise but unjust to test their opinions, and their social habits, by the standards of our time. No intelligent student of their history will ignore the fact that the world has made marvelous progress since 1620. The belief in witchcraft was, I think, universal in Christendom in that age. The great jurists and philosophers of England were confident that there were such creatures as witches. Sir Matthew Hale, and Sir Thomas Browne, and Ralph Cudworth, and Blackstone, and even John Wesley believed in witchcraft. "It is supposed," says Professor Fisher, "that prior to the witchcraft epidemic in Massachusetts, thirty thousand persons had been put to death in England on this charge, seventy five thousand in France, and a hundred thousand in Germany."[1]

Cruel punishments were inflicted in the times of Queen Elizabeth. She sent Mary Queen of Scots to the block, just as Charles the Second sent Sir Henry Vane to the block. The spirit of our age does not tolerate slavery, but slavery was common then. Our societies for the Prevention of Cruelty to Animals; Cruelty to Children; the laws that protect children and women from excessive labor; that prohibit cock-fighting, and prize-fighting, and, in some States, prohibit bull-fighting, — all these are the outgrowths of the last years of the nineteenth century. We do not look for such things in the times of Oliver Cromwell.

It is not easy for us to do justice to an age so different from our

---

[1] George Park Fisher, *History of the Christian Church* (London: Hodder and Stoughton, 1890), 479.

own. Life was more simple in those days, yet in many ways it was more picturesque, more courtly, more reverent. The respect that was paid to parents, and to the aged, and to those in official positions, the reverence for the Bible, and the Church, and the Lord's-day, the interest in philosophy and theology, and in religious services, — these were very unlike the tendencies of our time.

It does not follow that the life of that time was inferior to the life of today. Those people were evidently sincere in the expression of their opinions. Their manners and methods of life grew out of their experiences. The habits of Queen Elizabeth were very different from those of Queen Victoria, yet it may be that Elizabeth's place in history is higher than Victoria will deserve. Our nineteenth century has no poets or dramatists to be compared with Milton and Shakespeare. Certainly, we have no reason to look down upon the men who lived in the times of John Hampden, and Eliot, and Pym, and Vane, and Milton, and Cromwell. Mr. Gladstone has recently said: "I do not think we are stronger, but weaker, than the men of the Middle Ages. The men of the sixteenth century were stronger in brain power than our men."[2]

---

2 William Thomas Stead, "Mr. Gladstone - Part I: The Too Great Orb of Our Fate," *Review of Reviews Volume 5*, April, 1892, 360.

4

EVERYDAY LIFE IN PLYMOUTH AND THE COLONIES

•

The Colony at Plymouth

WE should also remember that the fathers of New England were pioneers. Those who make the first settlements in a new country cannot live as they had lived in their old homes. Many of the criticisms upon the Puritans are very inconsiderate. They have been spoken of as hard and narrow, because they did not have days of public festivity and amusement.

But the settlers at Plymouth had to build houses to shelter their families, with their own hands, in the depth of winter. They had no domestic animals except dogs. They had no ploughs. They must break up the land, and prepare it for corn with hoes. "The first beginning of any cattle in the land," says Bradford, "was in March, 1624, when three heifers and a bull were landed."[1] For three years and more the Colony had been without milk or butter or cheese except such as came from abroad.

All their journeys were on foot or in boats. There was often great scarcity of food. There were no preserved meats, no vegetables, and

---

1 William Bradford, *History of Plymouth Plantation* (Boston: Little Brown, 1856), 158.

no bread stuffs to be had. Water was the only drink, except beer and liquors. There was a time when lobsters, clams, and mussels furnished the principal food of the people. After the return of Governor Winslow from England, they were able to allow four ounces of bread a day to each inhabitant, and this was given out each day. Two years after the settlement was begun, two ships arrived from England, bringing a large number of the wives and children of the earliest settlers, who had been left behind at Leyden. It was a joyful reunion, and yet the new-comers "found their old friends in a very low condition; many were ragged in apparel, and some little better than half naked. The best dish they could present their friends with was a lobster, or a piece of fish, without bread, or anything else but a cup of pure spring water."[2] "The long continuance of this diet," says Governor Bradford, "and their labors abroad had somewhat abated the freshness of their former complexion." The fact is, the new-comers hardly recognized their own kindred, so changed were they by the lack of nutritious food, and by the severity of their labors. Governor Bradford compares their condition to that of Jacob and his sons in Canaan, in the time of famine. For, he says, although "the famine was great, or heavy in the land; yet they had such great herds, and store of cattle of sundry kinds, which, besides flesh, must needs produce other food, as milk, butter and cheese, etc., and yet it was counted a sore affliction; theirs here must needs be very great, therefore, who not only wanted the staff of bread, but all these things, and had no Egypt to go to. But God fed them out of the sea for the most part, so wonderful is his providence over his in all ages; for his mercy endureth for ever."[3]

In addition to these troubles, the Colony was in debt to the company in England, which had provided the vessel that brought them over,

---

2 Ibid., 145-146.
3 Ibid., 146.

and the supplies for the settlers. For many years they were obliged to send to England, whatever they had gained from their trade with the natives, towards the payment of their debts. Besides this, they had among them a number of persons who were not honest or industrious men. Some of those who were sent over by the company in England were so bad that they were obliged to send them back at large expense. All through the history of the Plymouth Colony they had to carry along with them a good many people who had no sympathy with the high moral standards of the Pilgrims.

They were also exposed to attacks from the savages about them. They treated the Indians with great kindness and consideration; but they were never free from the danger of a hostile attack. Their village was protected by a line of palisades, with bastions; and the gates were locked at night and guarded. They built a fort, on the top of which they planted six cannon. In times of special danger, a watch was kept up at the fort day and night.[4] As the years went by, their hardships were less, but their condition was still that of pioneers, in a new country, with the ocean between them and the old home.

The Massachusetts Colony

The larger Colony at Massachusetts Bay was better provided for. The first ships that came over brought with the passengers, cows, horses, goats, and swine.[5] They had also a supply of provisions. And yet, more than a quarter of those who came to Salem died during the first winter. Two hundred of Governor Winthrop's company died before the close of the autumn. There was great suffering from the lack of food, in the winter that followed. Shellfish had to serve for meat, and ground-nuts and acorns for bread. The rude cabins which the people

---

4 Ibid., 113, 126.

5 John Gorham Palfrey, *History of New England Volume I* (Boston: Little Brown, 1859), 223.

were able to put up were a very poor protection against the cold of a New England winter, for people, many of whom had lived in great comfort in the old country. "Oh the hunger that many suffered," said one of the old writers, "and saw no hope to be supplied, only by clams, and muscles, and fish."[6] When the first ship arrived from England, with provisions for the Colony, Governor Winthrop was giving the last handfuls of meal in the barrel to a poor man.

These settlements were also subject to alarms from bands of hostile Indians who were prowling about.[7] A few years later, they had occasion to fortify the harbor of Boston, and arm and drill the men of the Colony, because they had reason to expect a hostile attack from the king's ships. The colonies in Rhode Island, and Connecticut, and New Hampshire had a similar record of privation and suffering during the first years. In the course of time the industry and thrift of the people brought them such comforts and such prosperity as can be had in new settlements. But life in New England was very simple for many years. In 1632, Governor Winthrop records the removal of the windmill from Newtown to Boston, because at Newtown it would not grind but with a westerly wind. The whole Colony seems to have been dependent upon a single windmill.[8]

The next year, a watermill was set up in Dorchester, and another in Roxbury. The same year a "Mercate" (Market) was authorized to be kept on Thursday, in Boston, "it being lecture day." The long journeys which Governor Winthrop made on the business of the Colony were on foot, or in boats, for many years. When he visited Plymouth, Governor Bradford, — "a very discreet and grave man," — with Mr. Brewster the Elder, and some others came forth and met them without

---

6 Roger Clap, *Memoirs of Roger Clap* (Boston: David Clapp, Jr., 1844), 30.
7 John Winthrop and James Savage, *The History of New England from 1630 to 1649 Volume 1* (Boston: Phelps and Farnham, 1825), 55.
8 Ibid., 87.

the town, and conducted them to the house of the Governor, where they were very kindly entertained, and feasted each day at several houses. On Wednesday following, "the Governor and his company came out of Plymouth about five in the morning; the Governor of Plymouth, with the pastor and Elder, etc., accompanying them near half a mile, out of town, in the dark."[9]

In the second generation, as almost always happens in a new country, the people in the New England colonies were, as a class, of ruder manners, and of a lower grade of intelligence than those who had come from the Mother Country. There was some improvement in the third generation; but all through the first century of our history, the people had the characteristics of pioneers. It is not reasonable for the critics of our time to expect from these pioneers, of two hundred and sixty years ago, the broad and liberal views, and the generous culture of their descendants of the seventh generation.

Longfellow's *The Courtship of Miles Standish*

Mr. Longfellow's poem, entitled, "The Courtship of Miles Standish," gives us a very correct picture of the social and family life of the Pilgrims. The poet was interested in the tradition on which the poem is founded from family reasons.

It is not claimed that this poem is in all respects accurate in its statements. It is a work of art; and the poet has grouped about the central story a number of incidents which occurred in a little different connection. John Alden was not quite the youngest of those who came in the Mayflower, though he was a young man of twenty-one. Rose Standish was not the first of those who died at Plymouth. The milk-white steer, which, according to the poem, carried the bride on its back, to her new home, after the simple marriage ceremony,

---

9 Ibid., 92.

was doubtless still in Old England when the marriage occurred, two years after the Mayflower went back. But after all the liberty which we have to allow to the poet, it remains true that this poem gives a correct representation of the spirit of the Pilgrims, and of their way of life in 1623. The journals of Mr. Longfellow show that he was a diligent student of the early New England history at the time he was writing the poem.[10] The characters in the poem are well-known persons in the history of the Colony. Miles Standish was such a man as the poet has described, even to the books in his library, a catalogue of which has been preserved.[11] John Alden is a typical Pilgrim, with a warm heart, a high sense of honor, a vigilant conscience, and the imagination of an enthusiastic leader of men. He became a leading man in the Colony, was one of the Assistants more than forty years, treasurer of the Colony thirteen years, and was frequently a deputy to the General Court. Priscilla Mullins, — "the beautiful Puritan maiden," the lover of music,—

> Singing the hundredth Psalm, the grand old Puritan anthem...
> While with her foot on the treadle she guided the wheel in its motion.
> Open wide on her lap, lay the well-worn psalm-book of Ainsworth,
> Printed in Amsterdam, the words and the music together,
> Rough-hewn, angular notes, like stones in the wall of a churchyard.

Governor Bradford, also, is faithfully represented in the poem. So is Elder Brewster, though he was not so aged a man, at the date of the marriage, as the poet would have him.

---

10 Samuel Longfellow, *The Life of Henry Wadsworth Longfellow Volume 2* (Boston: Houghton Mifflin, 1893), 289-320.

11 John Abbot Goodwin, *The Pilgrim Republic: An Historical Review of the Colony of New Plymouth* (Boston: Houghton Mifflin, 1899), 150-151.

The tradition on which the action of the poem is founded, is certainly very old. It is probably authentic. It is very likely that the bashful captain — "A man not of words, but of actions," and "A maker of war, and not a maker of phrases" — was so indiscreet as to send his youthful secretary to ask for the hand of the young woman, who was...

...alone in the world; her father and mother and brother
Died in the winter together.

Her reply, according to the best tradition, was, "Why so many words for the Captain, and no words for yourself, John?"

The charm of the poem for us is in its picture of the life at Plymouth. What can be finer than the description of the departure of the Mayflower? —

Long in silence they watched the receding sail of the vessel,
Much endeared to them all, as something living and human;
Then, as if filled with the spirit, and wrapt in a vision
prophetic,
Baring his hoary head, the excellent Elder of Plymouth
Said, "Let us pray!" and they prayed, and thanked the Lord and
took courage.
Mournfully sobbed the waves at the base of the rock, and above
them
Bowed and whispered the wheat on the hill of death, and their
kindred
Seemed to awake in their graves, and to join in the prayer that
they uttered.

Here is the new Pilgrim home: —

Meanwhile Alden at home had built him a new habitation,
Solid, substantial, of timber rough-hewn from the firs of the
forest.
Wooden-barred was the door, and the roof was covered with rushes;
Latticed the windows were, and the window-panes were of paper,
Oiled to admit the light, while wind and rain were excluded.
There too he dug a well, and around it planted an orchard:

Oft when his labor was finished, with eager feet would the
dreamer
Follow the pathway that ran through the woods to the house of
Priscilla,
Led by illusions romantic and subtile deceptions of fancy,
Pleasure disguised as duty, and love in the semblance of
friendship.

Ever of her he thought, when he fashioned the walls of his
dwelling;
Ever of her he thought, when he delved in the soil of his garden;
Ever of her he thought, when he read in his Bible on Sunday
Praise of the virtuous woman, as she is described in the
Proverbs.

This was the wedding morn of Priscilla the Puritan maiden.
Friends were assembled together; the Elder and Magistrate also
Graced the scene with their presence, and stood like the Law and
the Gospel,
One with the sanction of earth and one with the blessing of
heaven.

Simple and brief was the wedding, as that of Ruth and of Boaz.

Softly the youth and the maiden repeated the words of betrothal,

Taking each other for husband and wife in the Magistrate's presence,

After the Puritan way, and the laudable custom of Holland.

Fervently then, and devoutly, the excellent Elder of Plymouth

Prayed for the hearth and the home, that were founded that day in affection,

Speaking of life and of death, and imploring Divine benedictions.

When all was over we read:

Onward the bridal procession now moved to their new habitation,

Happy husband and wife, and friends conversing together.

Pleasantly murmured the brook, as they crossed the ford in the forest,

Pleased with the image that passed, like a dream of love through its bosom,

Tremulous, floating in air, o'er the depths of the azure abysses.

Like a picture it seemed of the primitive, pastoral ages,

Fresh with the youth of the world, and recalling Rebecca and Isaac,

Old and yet ever new, and simple and beautiful always,

Love immortal and young in the endless succession of lovers

So through the Plymouth woods passed onward the bridal procession.

Schooling and Education

These records and traditions may help us to understand the social and family life of the Puritans. We pass next to *some of the practical methods by which these hardy pioneers directed their social and family life.* We are not to expect them to follow the conventional rules of the Old World. They were men of ideas and of independent principles. They had found it impracticable to develop their ideas in England. The Stuarts, and those who belonged to their party, had crowded these vigorous Protestants — the champions of civil and religious liberty — from their homes, and they had come to the New World to develop their ideas in a free state and a free Church. They were men far in advance of their times. Longfellow has borrowed the strong expression of one of their leaders, when he says:

God had sifted three kingdoms to find the wheat for this planting,
Then had sifted the wheat, as the living seed of a nation.[12]

The Puritans sought to develop the individual. As they believed that each man was the special object of God's love and care, so they insisted that each child should be educated and trained for his duties in this life and beyond. That was the reason why they provided schools for the children of the people. They had no examples of such schools in England. They were more than two centuries in advance of the Mother Country in this respect. "Until quite recently," says an English writer, "there was no public provision for education in England, and even now it is only the elementary education of the people that can be said to be regulated by law."[13] James Russell Lowell speaks of the founders of New England as the inventors of Common Schools, and

12 Henry Wadsworth Longfellow, *The Courtship of Miles Standish and Other Poems* (Boston: Ticknor and Fields, 1859), 54.
13 Edmund Robertson, "Education" in *Encyclopedia Britannica 9th Edition Volume 7* (Edinburgh: Adam and Charles Black, 1875), 679.

says that these schools are defenses against "monopoly in Church and state."[14] Sir William Berkeley, one of the early Governors of Virginia, wrote to England, "I thank God there are no free schools or printing, and I hope we shall not have them these hundred years. For learning hath brought heresy, and disobedience, and sects into the world, and printing hath divulged them, and libels against the best government. God keep us from both."[15]

The Dutch Republic, however, had an excellent system of common schools; and when the Pilgrims went to Leyden, they found a land "where every child went to school, where almost every inhabitant could read and write."[16] Governor Bradford tells us that they were at first unable to establish a school at Plymouth, "for want of a fit person, and also for lack of means to pay a teacher." So the parents taught their own children to read in the first years; but, as soon as they were able, they set up common schools, and required all towns which had fifty families to maintain such schools. The Annals of the Colony are full of references to schools and schoolmasters.[17]

There was a school in Boston five years after the first settlement, of which Philemon Parment was the teacher. Daniel Maude was his successor, and for his maintenance a contribution of fifty pounds was made by the leading citizens. Governor Winthrop states that "divers free schools were erected, as at Roxbury, (for the maintenance whereof every inhabitant bound some house or land for a yearly allowance forever) and at Boston, where they made an order to allow forever fifty pounds to the master, and an house, and thirty pounds

14 James Russell Lowell, *Among My Books* (Boston: Houghton Mifflin, 1882), 242.
15 Douglas Campbell, *The Puritan in Holland, England, and America* (New York: Harper & Brothers, 1893), 32.
16 John Lothrop Motley, *History of the United Netherlands Volume 4* (London: John Murray, 1876), 399.
17 Bradford, *Plymouth Plantation*, 161-162. Goodwin, *Pilgrim Republic*, 494-497. *Records of the Town of Plymouth Volume 1 - 1636 to 1705* (Plymouth: Avery & Doten, 1889).

to an usher, who should also teach to read and write, and cipher; and Indians' children were to be taught freely. Other towns did the like, providing maintenance by several means."[18]

In 1647, a general act was passed, which required every town of fifty families or more, to appoint one to teach all children to read and write; and every town of one hundred families to set up a grammar school, the masters thereof being able to prepare students for the University. Ezekiel Cheever was the earliest schoolmaster in New Haven, and John Higginson the first in Hartford. Every New England Colony, as soon as it was able, provided for the support of schools; "to the end that learning may not be buried in the graves of our forefathers in Church and commonwealth." The movement for universal education was in the air in those years. Wherever the Puritans planted themselves, their social and family life was the life of readers and thinkers. The common school has gone to Virginia now, and far beyond, in disregard of the prayer of the old Tory Governor. The first settlers of these earliest American colonies, north and south, planted the seeds from which their descendants of the seventh generation are reaping. The schools for the people may have brought some heresies, and some disobedience, but they have brought light; they have brought free and liberal thought; they have brought liberty to the slaves, and help to the poor, and light to the ignorant. The common schools made possible the New England town-meeting, — that little congress of the local democracy which was the germ of the republic.

Legislation and Laws

The legislation of the Puritans also influenced their social life. Many of their laws, it is true, had the characteristics of the seventeenth

---

18 John Winthrop and James Savage, *The History of New England from 1630 to 1649 Volume 2* (Boston: Phelps and Farnham, 1825), 215.

century. But, as a whole, their legislation was far in advance of their times. It is common, even now, for writers of limited information to refer to the so called Blue Laws of Connecticut as specimens of the laws of the Puritans. It is said that the laws contained such provisions as these: No one shall travel, cook victuals, make beds, sweep house, cut hair, or shave on the Sabbath day. No woman shall kiss her child on the Sabbath or Fasting day; no one shall read the *Book of Common Prayer*, keep Christmas, or Saint days, make minced pies, dance, play cards, or play on any instrument of music, except the drum, trumpet, and Jew's Harp; no one shall run on the Sabbath day, or walk in the garden or elsewhere except reverently, to and from meeting; no food or lodging shall be afforded to a Quaker or other Heretic; every male shall have his hair cut round according to a cap.[19]

It is well known that these Blue Laws were the invention of one Samuel Peters, a Tory, who had been driven from the country on account of his disloyalty, during the war of the Revolution. He published in London, in 1781, a book which professes to give "A History of Connecticut from its first settlement." The code of laws which this book contains has been proved to be a fabrication. There were no such laws in Connecticut or in any other part of New England; "nor is there any record of so much as single judgment pronounced agreeably to the tenor of these provisions."[20]

Some of the laws which were enacted in New England were like those in force in other parts of the Christian world at that time. There were sumptuary laws everywhere; laws to punish those whose religious opinions were different from those of the majority; laws de-

19 Samuel Peters, *General History of Connecticut* (New York: D. Appleton, 1877), 57-61.

20 James Hammond Trumbull, *The True-Blue Laws of Connecticut and New Haven and the False Blue-Laws Invented by the Rev. Samuel Peters* (Hartford: American Publishing Company, 1876) and John Gorham Palfrey, *History of New England Volume 2* (Boston: Little Brown, 1865), 30-37.

signed to enforce religious duties; meddlesome laws, interfering with small matters, which it is wiser to let alone. There were cruel laws; laws which imposed the death-penalty for offenses which we have learned to deal with in another way.

But the laws of New England were more merciful than those of New York, or of Virginia. They were much more merciful than the laws of England. At the end of the reign of Queen Elizabeth, thirty-one crimes were punished with death by the laws of England. Connecticut had only twelve capital crimes in 1642, Massachusetts at the same date had ten, Plymouth had only eight.[21] In England, those who were adjudged guilty of the crime of witchcraft were to be put to death without benefit of clergy. The writ for burning a heretic (de haretico comburendo) was not abolished in England till late in the reign of Charles the Second. As late as the time of James the Second, fourteen hundred Quakers were in prison at one time in England, in accordance with the laws then in force in that country.[22] By the laws of Virginia, Quakers, or other Separatists who should join in religious worship not authorized in England or this country, were, for the third offense, to be banished from Virginia.[23] Quakers were to be put to death if they should return a second time. No minister was allowed to hold a religious service unless he had been ordained by a bishop in England. Any person absenting himself from divine service for a month was to be fined; and if he should refuse to pay his fine, he was to be whipped, "on the bare back, ten lashes, well laid on." The penalty for blasphemy, in Maryland, in 1649, was for the first offense to "be bored through the tongue," and for the third offense it was death.[24]

---

21 Ibid., and Ibid., 27-31. *The Colonial Laws of Massachusetts* (City of Boston, 1889), 29-68.
22 Edward Fry, "Quakers" in *Encyclopedia Britannica 9th Edition Volume 20* (Edinburgh: Adam and Charles Black, 1875), 147-153.
23 Thomas Jefferson, *Notes on the State of Virginia* (Richmond: J.W. Randolph, 1853), 168.
24 Trumbull, *True-Blue Laws and False Blue-Laws*, 309-360.

Some of these seventeenth century laws were enacted in the New England colonies. Some were put in a milder form; many were repealed or greatly modified in a few years. The decided tendency in these colonies was towards softening the penalties or repealing the laws. The reason was that the legislators that enacted all laws were elected by the people in their town-meetings, and these representatives were very susceptible to public opinion. The law which provided that Quakers who returned to the Colony after they had been banished should be put to death, was very unpopular among the people. It has been already stated that it was passed in the House of Deputies by a majority of one vote.[25] The penalty was executed upon four persons. But the pressure of public opinion against the law was so strong that after three or four years the law became a dead letter, and before many years it was repealed.

The prosecutions for witchcraft, in 1691 and 1692, were brought under an old law enacted fifty years before. While the excitement lasted, and within a limited area, juries were found that would convict on such poor testimony as was presented. But public opinion soon condemned the prosecutions, and within a few months it was impossible to find a jury that would bring in a verdict of guilty of Witchcraft. The people sent such remonstrances to the General Court that the prosecutions were stopped. It was the enlightened judgment of the Puritan Colonists that put a stop to these judicial murders, which were continued in Europe for many years afterwards.

The Puritan legislation was very practical. James Russell Lowell has spoken in emphatic terms of the practical good sense of our fathers. They had been the champions of liberty in England; and they adopted, very early, the *Body of Liberties*, prepared by Mr. Nathaniel Ward

---

25 Nathaniel Bradstreet Shurtleff, *Records of the Governor and Company of the Massachusetts Bay in New England Volume 4 - Part 1 1650-1660* (Boston: William White, 1854), 345-347.

of Ipswich, a man learned in the law, as well as in divinity, which stated in clear and vigorous terms the rights of the citizen under the law. "No man's life shall be taken away; no man's honor or good name shall be stained; no practical man's person shall be arrested, restrained, banished, or anyways punished; no man shall be deprived of his wife or children; no man's goods or estate shall be taken away, . . . unless by virtue of some express law of the country, established by the General Court and sufficiently published."[26]

The laws tended strongly toward democracy. They tended also to protect the family; to secure its purity and its permanence; to restrain vice and crime; to protect the poor and the weak. The laws regulated the sale of intoxicating drinks, perhaps as effectually as our modern laws have done. It is doubtful whether we have made any real progress in respect to that class of legislation, since the time of Governor Winthrop. For many years the General Court assumed the guardianship of widows and orphans, and the care of the insane and other unfortunate people. There were also laws to protect the Indians from injustice, as well as from the tendencies to vice from their contact with unprincipled white men. These laws were designed to aid the missionary work among them.

Aristocratic Traditions

Life in New England was less democratic in the Colonial period than it is in our time. Many of the class distinctions of old England were transferred to the new country. Only twelve of those who came in the Mayflower had the title Mr. prefixed to their names. The others were plain John Alden, Thomas Williams, etc. Only a few of those in the Massachusetts Colony had the prefix Mr., or Mrs. These titles were given to those who had belonged to the class of gentlemen in England,

---

26 *Colonial Laws of Massachusetts*, 29-68.

and also to ministers, and physicians, and their wives. Goodman and goodwife were the appropriate addresses of persons who were below the condition of gentility, and above that of servants. Most of the deputies to the General Court were designated by their names only, unless they had a military title. A gentleman might be deprived of his rank for a disgraceful act. It was ordered by the Court, in 1631, that Josias Plastowe shall be fined five pounds for stealing corn from the Indians, and that hereafter he shall be called by the name of Josias, and not Mr. as formerly he used to be.[27] These distinctions in social rank were carefully preserved in the early catalogues of Harvard College. Those who had been graduated from College were entitled to the title Sir, until they had received the degree of Master of Arts, when their proper title was "Mister." People were sometimes seated in the meeting-house according to their social rank. Still, the tendency was towards a free and hearty life, as it is always in a new country. Conventional distinctions faded away, although there were traces of the aristocratic traditions they had brought from England, down to the time of the American Revolution.

---

27 Palfrey, *History of New England Volume I*, 352.

5

PURITAN CULTURE, ARTS AND ENTERTAINMENT

•

Dress

THE dress of the people during the Colonial period was generally plain, as well because of their limited resources, as because it was the policy of the colonies to discourage the wasting of their resources by habits of extravagance. And yet those in official positions were frequently passing to and from England, and it was necessary for them to maintain the style and manners of gentlemen of their rank in the old country. Professional men and public officers were expected to wear a distinctive dress. The typical Puritan, as his appearance is preserved in the old portraits, and in modern statues, looks like a man of distinction. Clothes counted for quite as much in the seventeenth century, as they do now.

The Simple Cobler of Aggawam in America complained of five or six extravagant women in the Colony, who inquire "what dress the Queen is in this week," and "what is the very newest fashion of the Court," and who "egge to be in it in all haste, whatever it be." "I honor the woman," he says, "that can honor herself with her attire, but for a woman who lives but to ape the newest court fashions I look at her as the very gizzard of a trifle, — the product of a quarter of a cipher, — the epitome of nothing."[1]

The General Court enacted laws at various times to limit extravagance in dress. The fact that such laws were needed shows that human nature in the times of the Puritans was very much the same that it is now. Their young people had a love for beautiful things; and they sought to adorn themselves, even beyond their means. The younger generation were not inconoclasts. Some of them were disposed to break away from the customs of the pioneers. In 1634, it was enacted that "no person, either man or woman, shall hereafter make or buy any apparel that hath lace in it, or silver and gold." It was afterward ordered that no one whose estate is less than two hundred pounds shall wear gold or silver lace, or gold or silver buttons. Still later, it was enacted that no one shall wear embroidered caps, gold and silver girdles, immoderate great sleeves, or slashed apparel.[2] We read in the *Records of the Colony of New Plymouth* of a man who created a sensation by appearing in the streets of Plymouth in long red-silk stockings.[3] In the inventory of the estate of plain Elder Brewster, we find "one blue cloth coat," one "violet color cloth coat," "one green waistcoat." In *New England's First Fruits* it is said, "Linen fustian we are making already; sheep are coming on for woolen cloth; in the meantime we may be supplied by way of trade from other parts; cordovan deer, seal, and moose skins are to be had plentifully, which will help this way, especially for servants' clothing."[4] Evidently these pioneers were thrifty people, who respected themselves, and dressed as well as they were able, though they avoided with prudent care habits that were

---

1 Nathaniel Ward, *The Simple Cobler of Aggawam in America* (Boston: James Munroe, 1843), 26.
2 Nathaniel Bradstreet Shurtleff, *Records of the Colony of New Plymouth in New England Volume 3 1644-1657* (Boston: William White, 1855), 243.
3 Shurtleff, *Records of New Plymouth Volume 1 1633-1640*, 93.
4 *New England's First Fruits* (London: Henry Overton, 1643), 44.

beyond their incomes.

Furniture

The inventory of the estate of Elder Brewster shows that his furniture was appraised at about one hundred pounds. The inventory of the household goods of Governor Winthrop sums up the value at one hundred and three pounds. This included several feather beds and bolsters worth two pounds apiece; a down bed, pillows and bolsters worth five pounds; a large number of pewter dishes and plates, tin plates, brass and copper kettles, brass candlesticks, brass and iron andirons, some old armor, fire-arms, several small carpets, cushions, cloaks, cloth-of-gold scarf, table-cloths, napkins, a large number of chairs, tables, cabinets, chests, two suits of clothes worth six pounds, six pairs of spectacles, and many other things.

There is preserved in the *Records of the Colony of Massachusetts*,[5] an inventory of the household goods of Mrs. Martha Coytmore, who afterwards became the fourth wife of Governor Winthrop. The whole value of the estate of her first husband seems to have been about thirteen hundred pounds. One hundred and twenty seven pounds of this was represented by the household furniture. The items are much the same as those in the inventory of the furniture of the Governor. Some articles, however, were more expensive. There was a cypress chest worth two pounds ten shillings, diaper table-cloths, with napkins, worth several pounds, a silk red and green quilt, striped curtains, and some silver plate worth fifteen pounds.

These are specimens of the inventories of the estates of persons in the best condition in life, in Boston, twenty years after the town was settled. The furniture in the largest number of houses was much more

---

5 Nathaniel Bradstreet Shurtleff, *Records of the Colony of New Plymouth in New England Volume 4 Part 1 - 1650-1660* (Boston: William White, 1854), 281.

primitive and of less cost.

Amusements

The amusements of these plain people dwelling in the wilderness were few and simple. And yet they were not as few as some writers would lead us to suppose. It is true that games of chance were prohibited by law. No one was permitted to possess cards, dice, or other instrument of gaming. Dancing was also prohibited.[6] But it is possible for the right sort of people to lead a pleasant social life without gaming or dancing.

The Puritans enjoyed their religion. They delighted in prayer, and in communion with God. They were profoundly interested in religious truth. Religious services were very attractive to them. They were intellectual people. The religious spirit has been found to agree very well with the intellectual spirit. The independent thinkers of New England, as a rule, had a Puritan ancestry.

Our fathers loved their new country, as pioneers generally do. They believed it was better than any other. They were free to work out their own ideas in this new world. They were readers and thinkers. They debated great questions under the shadows of the primitive forests. They did not feel the need of the pleasures which people of less intellect and less faith seem to require.

There is abundant evidence that there was a genuine, hearty, social life in these colonies. Travelers of that period, who came to New England, do not speak of the life they found here as a gloomy life. The people were interested in each other. They had their own simple rustic amusements such as those to which they had been accustomed in England.

Take as an example the first Harvest Festival at Plymouth. The

---

6 Shurtleff, *Records of New Plymouth Volume 3,* 224.

Pilgrims had gathered their first harvest, after the year of severe labor and privation, while they were building their houses, and breaking up the ground, and caring for their crops. The harvest was bountiful, and they had at last a right to give themselves up to recreation. We read, in *Mourt's Relation*:

> Our harvest being gotten in, our Governor sent four men on fowling, that we might after a more special manner rejoice together, after we had gathered the fruit of our labors. They four in one day killed as much fowl, as, with a little help beside, served the Company almost a week, at which time amongst other Recreations, we exercised our Arms, many of the Indians coming amongst us, and amongst the rest, their greatest King, Massasoyt, with some ninety men, whom for three days we entertained and feasted, and they went out and killed fine deer, which they brought to the Plantation, and bestowed on our Governor, and upon the Captain, and others.[7]

This was not a religious festival. There is no mention of any religious services. The week seems to have been given up to sports, and a succession of festivals, as well as to the entertainment of their dusky neighbors. In these ways, these vigorous men enjoyed themselves, making the best use of their limited opportunities.

In Massachusetts, there was a larger population, and a greater variety of occasions of interest. The house of Governor Winthrop was seldom without its guests. There were interesting people coming from abroad, whose presence added interest to the home-life. The

---

7 Henry Martyn Dexter, *Mourt's Relation or Journal of the Plantation at Plymouth* (Boston: John Kimball Wiggin, 1865), 133.

Commencement week at the new college was always interesting. We read of a great training on Boston Common, which brought together the people from the various settlements. Many gentlemen and gentlewomen dined in tents on the Common. Judge Sewell, in his *Diary*, refers very often to the dinner parties which he attended. He sometimes gives us the names of the guests, and tells us something of the bill of fare. The picture of a New England Holiday, in the "Scarlet Letter," with its mingled light and shade, gives a very fair impression of life in those days. Hawthorne says, very truly, that the generation next to the early emigrants — who had never mingled in the sports of Old England — wore the darkest shade of Puritanism.[8]

Human nature in the colonies was very much like human nature in the rest of the world. The amusements of the young people were not always such as their fathers and mothers approved. There are numerous records of "Mixed dancing, unlawful gaming, extravagance in dress, light behavior," and such like offenses. These things do not appear to have been confined to any one period in our history. They became more frequent as the colonies became richer and more populous. The family discipline was careful and faithful, but the habits and characters of the children did not always develop according to the Puritan model.

---

8 Nathaniel Hawthorne, *The Scarlet Letter* (Boston: James R. Osgood, 1878), 284. In some of his other books, Mr. Hawthorne fails to do justice to the Puritans.

6

THE PURITANS AND
THE FRENCH CATHOLICS

•

WE may draw another class of illustrations of the social life of the
Puritans from their intercourse with the French, whose settlements in
the north were older than those of the Puritans. The French officials
were zealous Roman Catholics, and their habits were very different
from those of the Puritans.

In 1643, La Tour arrived in Boston harbor with his ship, and a
hundred and forty people, among them two Friars, and two women
who were to wait upon the wife of La Tour. They were courteously
received by Governor Winthrop, who escorted La Tour to his lodgings on shore, "with a sufficient guard." While the Frenchmen were
in the town the training day came on, and La Tour witnessed with
pleasure the evolutions of the citizen-soldiers. In the afternoon, the
French soldiers were landed, with their arms, and they were permitted to exercise, "The Governor and others of the Magistrates coming
into the field." The Puritan soldiers escorted the Frenchmen to the
landing-place. "Our Governor and others in the town," we are told,
"entertained La Tour and his gentlemen with much courtesy, both in
their houses and at table. La Tour came duly to our church meetings,

and always accompanied the Governor to and from thence, who all the time of his abode here was attended with a good guard of halberts and musketeers." There were animated discussions among the people in regard to the propriety of receiving these "idolatrous Papists," as some called them, with so much honor. But the majority approved the wise and courteous course of the Governor. There was a good deal of social intercourse between the people and the French. We read:

> Of the two Friars which came in this ship, the one was a very learned acute man. Divers of our Elders, who had conference with him, reported so of him. They came not into the town, lest they should give offense, but once, being brought by some to see Mr. Cotton and confer with him, and when they came to depart, the chief came to take leave of the Governor, and the two Elders of Boston, and showed himself very thankful for the courtesy they found among us.[1]

This picture of the learned Friar, calling on John Cotton, to "confer with him," being brought by some of the Puritans, is one of the evidences that there was a place for courtesy toward those of another faith, among those stanch Protestants. Three years later, another company of Frenchmen came to Boston. They arrived on the Lord's-day.

> Major Gibbons sent two of his chief officers to meet them at the water side, who conducted them to their lodgings, *sine strepitu*. The public worship being ended, the Governor

---

1 John Winthrop and James Savage, *The History of New England from 1630 to 1649 Volume 2* (Boston: Thomas B. Wait and Son, 1826), 127.

repaired home, and sent Major Gibbons with a guard of musketeers to attend them to the Governor's house, who, meeting them without his door, carried them into his house, where they were entertained with wine and sweetmeats, and after a while, he accompanied them to their lodgings. The Governor explained to them the Puritan way of observing the Lord's-day, 'that all men either come to our public meetings, or keep themselves quiet in their houses.' The French Catholics complied with the customs of the Colony, for 'they continued private all that day until sunset, and made use of such books, Latin and French, as the Governor had, and the liberty of a private walk in his garden, and so gave no offense.' When they had finished their business, they were attended to their boat by the Governor, and the Commissioners of the Colony. When they sailed for home, they were saluted with five guns from Boston, three from Charlestown, and five from Castle Island. They returned the salute, and went of their voyage.[2]

A still more interesting incident occurred four years later. Father Gabriel Druillette, a Jesuit missionary among the Abenaquis, in what is now the State of Maine, was sent by the Governor of Canada, D'Ailleboust, as a diplomatic agent to Massachusetts, and to Plymouth. His purpose was to engage the Colonies in alliance with the French, against the Iroquois. The Jesuit missionary hoped by such an alliance to secure protection for the Christian Indians, against their savage enemies. He has left a journal of his visit, in French, which was published some forty years ago.[3]

---

2 Ibid., 273-275.
3 Gabriel Dreuillette, *Narré du voyage faict pour la mission des Abnaquiois et des connaissances tiréz de la Nouvelle Angleterre et des dispositions des magistrats de cette république pour le secours contre les Iroquois, ès années 1648 & 1649.*

Druillette reached Boston in December, 1650. He was known as a zealous Jesuit missionary. He was received with great courtesy and respect. He was invited to the house of General Gibbons, who charged him to make no other house his home, while he remained there. The General gave to his guest a key to an apartment in his house, where he might be free to pray, and to go through the services of his religion. It has been suggested that the first Mass in Boston may have been solemnized in that room. General Gibbons presented his guest to Governor Dudley, who examined his credentials, and invited him to dine at his house. From Boston, Father Druillette went to Plymouth, where he was courteously received by Governor Bradford, who invited him to dine at his house the next day. As the next day was Friday, the Pilgrim Governor provided fish for dinner, in recognition of the religious customs of his Jesuit guest. The Priest found favor among the people of Plymouth, although the Magistrates did not embarrass themselves by entering into the alliance which he proposed. On the 24th of December, the good missionary started on his return to Boston by land. On his way back, he called at Roxbury on John Eliot, the Puritan missionary among the Indians. It must have been about the time of Christmas day. He writes in his journal that Eliot invited him to lodge with him, as the night had overtaken him. These two missionaries — the Jesuit, and the Puritan — had much discourse concerning their work among the Indians. "Here is a scene," says Dr. Ellis, "that might well engage the pencil of an artist. These two men . . . separated as the poles in their religious convictions, principles and methods, are seen in simple, human, loving converse, as kind host, and responsive stranger guest. The humble sitting and working room of the Apostle Eliot, in his modest cottage, has the essentials of comfort, and there is a guest chamber." The Priest writes in his journal that Eliot treated him with respect and affection, and invited him to pass the winter with him. "Perhaps their conversation was in Latin," says Dr. Ellis, "though Eliot was an accomplished scholar, and might have the mastery of the French. The morning and evening devotions of the Puritan household, with grace and blessing each meal must have kept their wonted course, while the faithful Priest had his oratory, — his orisons, — and his matin Mass before breaking his fast."[4]

So nearly do good people of different creeds approach each other, who are devoted to the service of the one Lord, and to the salvation of their fellow-men.

---

4 John Gorham Palfrey, *History of New England Volume 2* (Boston: Little Brown, 1860), 308. George Edward Ellis, *The Puritan Age and Rule in the Colony of Massachusetts Bay 1629-1685* (Boston: Houghton Mifflin, 1888), 371.

7

PURITAN CULTURE
TODAY

•

THE last of all, we can estimate the social and family life of the Puritans, from its results, in the types of character which we find in their descendants. We are living among people of the seventh and eighth generation from the founders of New England. That is a long period through which to transmit distinctive traits. Mr. Galton, in his work *Hereditary Genius*, tells us that "the ablest race of whom history bears record is unquestionably the ancient Greeks."[1] But the Greek type, which was preserved for a few centuries, became gradually feebler, and was long ago lost. The Patricians at Rome were as distinctly marked in their time, but Gibbon tells us that at the time of the Republic most of the Patrician families had failed, and that the type was lost. Mr. Benjamin Kidd states that,

> Only five out of over five hundred of the oldest aristocratic families in England, at the present time, can trace direct descent through the male line, to the fifteenth century. Despite the immeasurable safeguards with which they have

---

1 Francis Galton, *Hereditary Genius: An Inquiry into Its Laws and Consequences* (London: Macmillan, 1869), 340.

been able to surround themselves, such classes seem to be quite unable to keep up the stock for more than a limited number of generations. They are continually dying out at the top, and being recruited from below.[2]

A similar state of things has been found to exist in France among the noble families of that country.

The Puritan type in this country has met a number of other vigorous types, each of which has molded a large number of our people. Beside the Cavaliers of Virginia, who made the Church of England the established Church in that Colony, there has been the Scotch, and the Scotch-Irish type, out of which has come the great Presbyterian Body. The French Huguenots have been very numerous. So have the Dutch, and the Germans. There has been a mingling of blood. Each type has exerted an influence upon the others, and there is a tendency to melt down these distinctive types in the comprehensive national spirit and character.

But for all that, the New England type of mind, after two hundred and seventy years, is still as distinct in the great stream of our American life, as the Gulf Stream in the Atlantic. A large fraction of the people of the United States have sprung from those who settled the colonies of New England. They are to be found in every State, and in almost every city and town. The men and women of Puritan blood, wherever we find them, are apt to be people of vigorous intellects, of thrifty habits, of inventive genius, and of strong moral character. They stand for liberty in the Church, and in the state. The leaders of liberal thought have been descendants of the Puritans. A large proportion of the great conservative leaders have also been of Puritan lineage. I find these men in the South, and in the extreme

2 Benjamin Kidd, *Social Evolution* (New York: Macmillan, 1894), 258.

West, as well as in the East. They are preaching in California and in Oregon. They are Senators and Representatives from Colorado, and from Michigan; from Washington, and from Ohio; from Wisconsin and from Illinois. President John Adams and President John Quincy Adams, and the poet Longfellow were among the descendants of John Alden and of Priscilla Mullins. Ralph Waldo Emerson was of the eighth generation of Puritan ministers. Nathaniel Hawthorne was a descendant of William Hawthorne, who came to America with Governor Winthrop, and who settled in Dorchester, in 1630. James Russell Lowell was a descendant from Percival Lowell, a prosperous merchant, who settled in Newbury, in 1639, and of the long line of his successors, — merchants and lawyers and ministers.

I have before me, as I write, a list of a hundred and twenty-five men who have died within the last three years, and who were members of the New England Historic Genealogical Society of Boston. They were not selected men, excepting that they were especially interested in the history of New England families. The majority of them were residents of Massachusetts, but a large number lived in other parts of New England, and in other sections of the country, and some in foreign lands. There are among them descendants of the French Huguenots, of the Scotch, the Dutch, and the English. It has been found, from an examination of this list of a hundred and twenty-five members of this Society, who have died in 1893, 1894, and 1895, that about two-thirds of them were able to trace their descent from the Pilgrims or the Puritans of New England. The list includes such names as William Frederick Poole, the Librarian of Chicago, Joseph H. Stickney, a merchant of Baltimore, Thomas E. Proctor and Benjamin F. Nourse of Boston, both successful business men, and both descended from persons who were put to death in Salem at the time of the witchcraft delusion, Ex-Governor Oliver Ames, and

Frederick L. Ames, and Waldo Higginson, Moses Kimball, Gyles
Merrill of Haverhill, Warren Ladd of Providence, Judge Charles C.
Baldwin of Cleveland, Elisha C. Leonard of New Bedford, James R.
Newhall of Lynn, Dr. Henry Delevan Paine of Albany, Daniel Clapp,
Peter Butler, Peter Thacher, James W. Austin, Francis G. Pratt, and
many others of Boston. These are representative men, specimens of
the thousands of men in active life who are of Puritan descent, whom
one may meet from day to day in business or in professional life.

Phillips Brooks was one of these representative men, a descendant
on his father's side from Thomas Brooks, and on his mother's side
from George Phillips, the first minister of Watertown. Three generations ago one of the descendants of John Cotton became the wife of
the great grandfather of Phillips Brooks. So that he came from at least
three lines of Puritan ancestors, — Cotton, Phillips, and Brooks. He
showed what a well developed Puritan of the seventh generation may
become under favorable circumstances. Francis Parkman, LL.D.,
the eminent historian of the French in America, who died in 1893,
traced his family line to Elias Parkman, through a long succession
of ministers and men of letters. Judge Peleg Emery Aldrich, who
has only recently passed away, was only one of the many eminent
descendants of George Aldrich of early Puritan times. Henry Oscar
Houghton, the eminent publisher, was of the seventh generation from
John Houghton. Leverett Saltonstall was descended from Sir Richard
Saltonstall, the leader in the settlement of Watertown. He was the
sixth in lineal descent to graduate from Harvard College. Dr. Andrew
P. Peabody was a descendant of the seventh generation from Lieut.
Francis Peabody, and from a long line of New England ministers. Dr.
Alonzo A. Miner was of the seventh generation from Thomas Miner,
who came to Boston in 1630. Robert C. Winthrop, LL.D., so eminent
as a statesman, an orator, and an author, was of the sixth generation

from the great Puritan Governor, John Winthrop. There have been eminent men in every period of the history of the Winthrops, but none have been more admirable than the eminent man who has so lately passed away.[3]

The Puritan discipline was undoubtedly severe, but it trained men for heroic action. That social and family life of theirs is still bearing fruit. The Puritan type is very persistent. No other section of the Anglo-Saxon race has excelled the Puritans in the number of great men and of good men,— soldiers and statesmen and scholars, that it has produced. Whether the social and family life of the present generation in New England is likely to preserve the type for other generations is an interesting and important question.

---

3 *The New England Historical and Genealogical Register Volume 48 1894* (Boston: New England Historic Genealogical Society).

PART II - RELIGIOUS BELIEFS

•

8

REFORMED
PROTESTANTISM

•

WE shall fail to understand the Puritans unless we know what views they adopted in regard to religious truth. For their whole tone and spirit, and their methods of life, were the outgrowth of their religious opinions. Like a great poet of our time, "they believed in the soul, and were very sure of God." They knew that He was not far from every one of them. Duty to God was their highest rule. Religious motives had the largest place in their lives. They had crossed the sea that they might be free to follow their convictions of duty. The larger number of them had been in a condition of comfort in England; some of them had been affluent. The early years of the reign of Charles the First had been times of great prosperity for those who could fall in with the teachings of the Established Church and with the views of the court. But they had left their English homes behind them, that they might be free to follow their religious convictions.

The Puritans were, first of all, Protestants. They lived to protest against error and to bear witness to the truth. Their Protestantism was of that intense and aggressive type, which generations of conflict with the Church of Rome had developed.

As Protestants they appealed to the Bible as the only infallible rule of faith and of duty. They asserted its authority in opposition to that of the traditions of the Church. But, in the interpretation of the Bible they insisted upon the right of private judgment. They denied the right of the Church, or of the councils, to give them an interpretation of the Word. A Puritan was a man who submitted with meekness to the teaching of God's word, *as he understood it.*

As consistent Protestants, the Puritans gave great emphasis to the doctrine of justification by faith. They guarded very carefully, in their teachings, against the covenant of works. They would not admit that there was any merit, as a ground of justification, in the best actions of the holiest men.

The Puritans derived from their study of the Bible a new sense of the sanctity of the Lord's-day. It was from the Puritans that the English people learned to keep the first day of the week so strictly that, even now, their habits of Sabbath observance are in marked contrast with those of the other nations of Europe. The Puritan clergymen would surrender their livings sooner than sanction the proclamation of the king, which required the people to devote a part of the day to amusements. The King's *Book of Sports* served the purpose of separating the Puritans from the other classes of their countrymen. One of the leading motives in the great Puritan migration was the desire to establish the habit of the strict observance of the Lords-day among their children.

The whole tone and spirit of New England during the first generation was unworldly, to a remarkable degree. There was a good deal of propriety in calling their state a theocracy. The sermons of the seventeenth century were longer and more abstract than those of our time. Many of them consisted of close and logical discussions of the doctrines of the Bible. Some of them were sections of theological treatises. Willard's *Body of Divinity* deserves to rank high among the theological works of New England; but it consists of two hundred and forty-six sermons. The first of them was preached January 31, 1687; the last, April 1, 1707, — an interval of twenty years. John Norton's theological works were given to his people in the form of sermons. So were those of John Cotton and of Thomas Hooker.

The few books which the Colonists were able to have in their homes were, for the most part, theological. They became as skillful as the Scottish people in theological discussion. They were as quick to detect any departure from the standards of doctrine which they had accepted, as the Athenians were to detect faults of pronunciation, or of style, in their orators. In those periods of their history there was good reason for the practice of preaching as candidates, for there were persons in every congregation who were qualified to form an intelligent opinion of the correctness of the teaching of the preacher. The great doctrines of religion were living themes for the people, the subjects of discussion at the fireside, in the market, and at all social gatherings.

Among Protestants, the fathers of New England belonged to the Reformed instead of the Lutheran branch of the Church, and to the Calvinistic instead of the Arminian party. The Pilgrims, who settled the Old Colony, had been trained under John Robinson, who was an able defender of the decrees of the Synod of Dort against the Arminians. The Puritans of the Bay Colony found the standards of the Westminster Assembly the best exponents of their faith. Up to the time of the Westminster Assembly, there does not seem to have been much discussion among them as to the particular shade of Calvinism they would teach. Their theology, like their religion, had been shaped by the hard experiences of their lives. It may be that the religion of the camp is not quite the same as that of the fireside. The

Puritans desired to exalt the sovereignty of God, for they believed He had chosen them for a great mission, and they depended utterly upon Him for protection and success. Many of those who had been driven from England had spent years in Geneva, and they had been influenced by the decided Calvinistic teachings of the ministers of that city. There was a difference among them, as to some points in the system, but the tendency during the first two generations was toward a very high type of Calvinism.

The books that were written in New England, in the first period, related to the organization and discipline of the churches, rather than to theology. "The Way of the Churches," "Necessity of Separation," "Why Ruling Elders Should Be Chosen," "The Necessity of Infant Baptism," "Should Those Not in Covenant with the Church Present Their Children for Baptism?" — these are specimens of the titles of the early pamphlets. When the Synod was convened at Cambridge, in 1646, it devoted itself to the Platform of Church Government, instead of the construction of a New Confession of Faith. The reason was that they were content, for the most part, to accept the Westminster Confession; but they felt the need of rounding out and completing that form of Church polity which had grown up in New England.

9

PURITAN THEOLOGY

•

THE Puritans were always, however, deeply interested in theology. What their views were, we may learn from the catechisms which they taught their children, as well as from the creeds of their churches, and from the books which they published.

For example, that famous catechism, prepared by John Cotton, in 1641 or 1642, at the request of the General Court, entitled "Milk for Babes," which was in common use for about a century, although it deals, for the most part, with practical matters of duty to God and to men, yet sets forth quite distinctly the doctrine of the Trinity, of the Fall of Man, asserting that "we sinned in Adam, and fell with him," and also that his sin is imputed to us; that the wages of sin is death; that "faith is a grace of the spirit whereby I deny myself, and believe on Christ for righteousness and salvation."

Also, the rhyming couplet in the *New England Primer*: "In Adam's fall, We sinned all," is not unlike the teachings of this catechism, in which several generations of Puritan children were trained.

Those who were admitted as members of the Puritan churches were required to give to the church an account of their religious experiences, and also of their "knowledge in the principles of religion." This "knowledge" included a statement of what truths and principles they had deduced from the Scriptures.[1]

It is clear from the early pamphlets that our fathers regarded the knowledge of the great principles of the Christian religion as an important preparation for admission to the church. The examination of the candidates as to their "knowledge of the principles of religion" led, in the course of time, to the adoption of a creed by the Church. Thus, the church in Salem, which was the earliest in New England, next to the Pilgrim church in Plymouth, had originally only this simple covenant: "We covenant with the Lord, and one with another: and do bind ourselves in the presence of God, to walk together in all his ways, according as he is pleased to reveal himself unto us in his Blessed word of truth."

As time went on, it was found expedient to expand this covenant, and make it more specific. In 1665, a formal creed was set forth with this title: *A Direction for a Public Profession in the Church Assembly, after Private Examination by the Elders: Which Direction Is Taken Out of the Scripture, and Points Unto That Faith and Covenant Contained in the Scripture; Being the Same for Substance Which Was Propounded to and Agreed upon by the Church of Salem in Their Beginning, the Sixth of the Sixth Month 1629.*

This ancient Confession of Faith sets forth the doctrine of the Trinity; of God's providence and government of the world; the fall of man; the redemptive work of Christ, who "became man that he might redeem and save us by his obedience unto death;" of the Holy Spirit; who, "working Faith in God's Elect, applyeth unto them Christ with all his Benefits of Justification, and Sanctification, unto Salvation."

---

1 These points are fully discussed by Williston Walker in *The Creeds and Platforms of Congregationalism* (New York: Charles Scribner, 1893), 106-107 and notes. He quotes the original authorities.

The history of the first Synod called by the General Court of Massachusetts, which met in what is now Cambridge, in 1637, gives some intimations of the discussions which went on among the Colonists in the earlier years.[2] Those were the days of Mrs. Hutchinson, who came to Boston in 1634. The questions which were raised by her bold teachings, set the whole Colony in a turmoil. The Synod chose Thomas Hooker, and Peter Bulkly as moderators, and proceeded to consider eighty-two erroneous opinions which had been set forth in this country at various times. One would think the Synod had abundant work on its hands, for the twenty-four days of its session. Most of these errors were traced to the teachings of Mrs. Hutchinson. It is plain that the intense religious spirit of the people had led them to speculate very freely with reference to the questions which had been raised by their new teachers. Some of their speculations were crude, and some, in the opinion of the Synod, were subversive to the fundamentals of religion. Cotton Mather states that they were of an Antinomian and Familistical tendency. The Synod dealt with these errors one by one.

After stating the erroneous opinions, they would say, "This is contrary to such and such texts of Scripture," and this, according to the author of the Magnalia, did "smite the error under the fifth rib." The influence of this Synod tended to harmonize the opinions of the people. In 1637, however, the General Court of Massachusetts banished Mrs. Hutchinson and some of her supporters from the Colony.[3]

About the time of the Westminster Assembly, there was, more or less dissent from some of the statements, which it was then common

---

2 John Winthrop and James Savage, *The History of New England from 1630 to 1649 Volume 2* (Boston: Phelps and Farnham, 1826), 269-271. Charles Francis Adams, *Three Episodes of Massachusetts History Volume 1* (Boston and New York: Houghton Mifflin, 1892), 468-475.

3 Cotton Mather, *Magnalia Christi Americana Volume 2* (Hartford: Silas Andrus, 1820), 443. Joseph Barlow Felt, *The Ecclesiastical History of New England Volume 1* (Boston: Congregational Library Association, 1855), 306-359. Walker, *Creeds and Platforms*, 132-135.

to make, in regard to the Atonement. Mr. Pynchon did not stand alone in his denial of the dogma of strict satisfaction. Some of the leading men among the Puritans in England were in sympathy with his views. But the larger number were against him. The reply to his book, by Mr. John Norton, asserted in the plainest terms that the Redeemer suffered the punishment which the sinner deserved to suffer. Mr. Norton did not hesitate to affirm that He suffered the torments of the souls that are lost. Both parties in this great debate imply that the Atonement of Christ is limited to the elect, and that there is no provision for the salvation of those whom God has not chosen unto salvation.

The meeting of the Cambridge Synod, in 1646 to 1648, was a very important event, not only because it led to the adoption of the Cambridge Platform of Church Government, but because the Synod adopted, for the first time, in the name of the churches of New England, a standard of doctrine. In the preface to the Platform the Synod declares: "We believe and profess the same Doctrine of the truth of the Gospel, which generally is received in all the reformed Churches of Christ in Europe: so especially, we desire not to vary from the doctrine of faith, and truth held forth by the Churches of our native country." It is further stated in this preface, that the Synod voted unanimously, "the last of the sixth month 1648, in these words: This Synod, having perused, and considered the Confession of faith published of late by the Reverend Assembly in England, do judge it to be very holy, orthodox, and judicious in all matters of faith: and do therefore freely and fully consent thereunto, for the substance thereof."[4]

These declarations of the Synod had an important influence upon the theological discussions of the New England divines for the next

---

4 Walker, *Creeds and Platforms,* 194-196.

half century, as we shall see from such of their works as have come down to us.

10

PURITAN THEOLOGICAL AND RELIGIOUS LITERATURE

•

WITHIN a few years after the time of the Cambridge Synod, a number of theological books were produced in New England, which were the first fruits of our literature, and which are the most authentic statements of the teachings of the early divines of New England.

Thomas Shepard

Thomas Shepard, the first pastor of the church in Cambridge, left a number of works which show how an active pastor, and an earnest preacher, understood the doctrines of the Gospel. Mr. Shepard was born in Northamptonshire, in 1605, received the degree of B.A. from Emmanuel College, Cambridge, in 1623, and that of M.A. in 1627. He received deacon's orders, and was appointed to one of the Puritan lectureships, in Essex, with a salary of 30 pounds a year.[1] He was permitted to labor in that place about three years and a half, when he was silenced by Bishop Laud, and driven out of the diocese. After incredible sufferings from persecution, during the next four years, he made his escape in disguise, and sailed for New England, in 1635. The

---

1 Thomas Shepard, *The Works of Thomas Shepard Volume 1* (Boston: Doctrinal Tract and Book Society, 1853), xii-xx, lxx-lxxi (see note on *Letters and Speeches by Oliver Cromwell*).

next year, the Church in Cambridge was formed, and Mr. Shepard was ordained as the first pastor. That was the year in which Harvard College was founded in Cambridge.

Mr. Shepard deserves to rank with Cotton, and Hooker, and Mather, among the leading ministers in the Colonies. His works belong to the first generation, for he died in 1649. "God's decree," he says, "is His eternal and determinate purpose concerning the effecting of all things, by His mighty power, according to His counsel." And yet, as a preacher, Mr. Shepard held to the freedom of the will. "In the fall," he tells us, "man abused his own free will, in yielding to the temptations which he might have resisted." The sin of Adam "is imputed unto us, and so the punishment must needs follow upon it."[2] He reasons in the usual manner in regard to this imputation. "We were in Adam, as the members are in the head, — as children in his loins, — as debtors in their surety, as branches in their roots: it being just that, as, if he standing, all had stood by imputation of his righteousness, — so, he falling, all should fall by imputation of his sin." So he declares that "every man living is born guilty of Adam's sin."[3] "The justice and equity is this: — All our estates were contained in that ship." "We were all in Adam, as a whole country is in a Parliament man, and though we made no agreement to have Adam stand for us, yet the Lord made it for us."

Passing next to Redemption, he tells us that, "It is the satisfaction made, or the price paid to the justice of God, for the life and deliverance of man out of the captivity of sin, Satan, and death, by a Redeemer, according to a covenant made between Him and the Father." So it came to pass that "Christ stood in the room of all them whom mercy decreed to save." "Justification is the gracious act of God, whereby, for

---

2 Ibid., 343.
3 Ibid., 24.

the satisfaction of Christ, apprehended by faith, and imputed to the faithful, He absolves them from the guilt and condemnation of all sin, and accepts them, as perfectly righteous, to eternal life." "Faith is the first act of our spiritual life, whereby, the soul, believing God, believeth in Him, and thus resteth, as in the only author and principle of life."[4] In this passage he teaches that faith is an act of the believer. So he taught that the sinner is free in his rejection of Christ. "The cause of this ruin," he says, "is from themselves." As a practical preacher, Shepard found it important to teach this truth with great earnestness. It is very plain, that those old Calvinistic preachers tried to develop a sense of freedom and of responsibility among those to whom they were preaching.

John Norton

The Orthodox Evangelist, by John Norton, of Ipswich, is one of the oldest elaborate theological works of the New England divines. It was published in London, in 1654. The original edition contains three hundred and fifty-five pages, and was written for the use of thoughtful laymen in the Puritan churches. The author was a preacher and pastor, as well as a well-read theologian. After a very subtle discussion of the essence of God, and of His attributes, he proceeds to His eternal decrees.

"The decree of God," he says, "is God's one, eternal, free, constant act, absolutely determining the infallible being of whatever is, besides Himself, unto the praise of His own glory." He says, with Calvin: "God willeth by one single act. With Him there is nothing past, — nothing to come, but all is present. Whatever He thinks, He always has thought, and always doth, and will think. There can no more be a

---

4 Ibid., 337, *Sum of the Christian Religion.*

new thought, or purpose, than a new God."[5] "The decree of God is the antecedent of sin, but it is not the cause of sin." "God is free from any motive besides His own will." "God is essentially good: —He is goodness itself." "All goodness cometh from Him." "God is a full fountain; willing to communicate of His goodness, as the sun communicates of its light."[6] "The will of God is the rule of justice between Him and His creatures. The holiness of God is conformity unto Himself."[7] "The justice of God leads Him to render unto the reasonable creature what is due thereunto, according to His word, whether by way of grace, or punishment."

In respect to man, he says: "The liberty of man, though subordinate to God's decree, freely willeth the very same thing, and no other, than that which it would have willed, had there been no decree. Man acts as freely as if there were no decree. Liberty is the effect of the decree; so far is the decree from being a hindrance to liberty."[8] In the same connection, he says: "All who hear the gospel, are equally bound to believe. How can God command those to believe, whom He hath decreed that they shall not believe?" "Hope is grounded upon God's revealed will, not upon the decree that is unrevealed." "Every person that heareth the gospel is equally capable of believing. We are to look upon all those living under the gospel as elected, in the judgement of charity. It is the duty of every one to believe."[9] "It is a sin for any to conclude in this life that he is among the reprobate."

He agrees with the other Calvinists of his time in respect to the fall of man, and the consequences of the fall. "Adam, being a public person, his posterity, in a seminal respect, was contained in his

---

5 John Norton, *The Orthodox Evangelist* (London: John Macock, 1654), 51-52.
6 Ibid., 13.
7 Ibid., 16.
8 Ibid., 76.
9 Ibid., 198-200.

loins, and so sinned in him sinning." "Adam might not have sinned; and yet, it could not be but that Adam should sin. Both of these are true."[10] "Necessity and liberty consist together." "God imputes the guilt of his sin to all his posterity." "Original sin is propagated in the soul by reason of the sin of Adam."[11] "The soul contracts sin, by its connection with the body, as when one falls into the dirt, he is defiled, and besmeared." "God, whiles He creates souls, doth deprive them of original righteousness."[12]

And yet he teaches that "the Parable of the Prodigal Son's return unto his father's house is proposed as the pattern of the sinner's being brought home unto Jesus Christ. The younger son was sensible of his lost condition before he was found."[13] Still, "the elect's seeking God, is the effect of God's seeking them. Our seeking before faith is the effect of the common work of the Spirit: our seeking after faith is the effect of the saving work of the Spirit."[14] "The Arminians tax the Orthodox for asserting all acts before faith to be sin; and they pretend that there is in man, before regeneration, a hunger and thirst, after righteousness, and a hatred of sin. They say that to all such God giveth sufficient grace to believe. But this is contrary to the Scripture."[15]

"Saving faith is an impulse or motion of the spirit of grace. It enables the soul to yield obedience unto the Commands of God."[16] "The soul is passive in vocation; that is, in the infusion of the principle of life."[17] "The manner of working of faith is irresistible, that is, it prevaileth over all opposition." But there are certain means of obtaining faith; such as "God's love to men, and Christ's work for sinners, and the invitations

10 Ibid., 74-75.
11 Ibid., 143.
12 Ibid.
13 Ibid., 138.
14 Ibid., 156-158.
15 Ibid., 166.
16 Ibid., 220.
17 Ibid., 257.

of the gospel."[18]

"Justification is a gracious act of God upon a believer, whereby he doth freely discharge him from sin, and accept him as righteous with the righteousness of Christ, and acknowledge him to have a right to eternal life. The efficient cause of Justification is the good pleasure of God."[19]

These citations are sufficient to show the method of this most logical of the early divines of New England. Undoubtedly, he held firmly the system of John Calvin, in all its essential points. And yet he sought constantly to guard against the tendency of that system to a denial of human freedom, and of personal responsibility. He made much of the free love of God, and of the motives of the Gospel. It is plain that his methods of thinking as a logician were very often modified by his moral instincts as a preacher.

Thomas Hooker

A greater man than John Norton, was the learned and accomplished Thomas Hooker, whose moving eloquence in the pulpit was equaled only by his statesmanship. Hooker was the author of a large number of religious books, which contain altogether more than two thousand pages. These were printed at various times between 1637 and 1651. One of them was printed in Amsterdam, the others in London. We find in these books the theology of Calvin, concerning the decrees, the fall of man, original sin, inability, irresistible grace, and the perseverance of the saints. This theology, however, is used in a practical way, and accommodated to the exigencies of the preacher. There are hints in these volumes of the distinction between natural and moral ability, which President Edwards brought out a hundred years later.

---

18 Ibid., 213-215.
19 Ibid., 300.

Hooker teaches that man is free, and therefore fully responsible. He makes much of the abounding love of God, and of the free and hearty offers of divine grace.

His longest work is entitled "The Soul's Vocation, or Effectual Calling to Christ," published in London in 1638, and contains six hundred and sixty-eight pages. He says,

> The offer of grace from God is free: the means of grace are also free: grace must be free because there is nothing in man to purchase it: and because he can do nothing to merit it. The saints should therefore magnify the mercy of God. The wicked, that want this mercy, should take encouragement, and seek after this mercy, seeing it is free. Those burdened under their sins should hope for mercy from the freeness of it. The soul must be willing to receive Christ and grace before it will have Christ and grace.[20]

"The will is the natural power or faculty wherewith every one is endowed to will." "The will is the hand of the soul. But the hand must turn towards the object, and open itself before it can grasp its object. So a man must turn his will towards an object and open itself. The hand of the soul must be open, before it can close with and fasten upon a thing. When the soul opens the hand to catch at grace, and lay hold thereupon, then it wills to receive grace. So, when we are unwilling to receive a thing, we turn away our hearts from the thing. When the soul is unwilling to receive anything, it shuts itself against that thing, and will by no means receive it."[21] "Whosoever in truth

20 Thomas Hooker, *The Soul's Vocation or Effectual Calling to Christ* (1638), 1-23. Extant copies of this were unable to be located by the publisher.
21 Ibid., 31.

doth will to have Christ, shall receive him."[22]

"No man, of himself, by nature, can will to receive Christ. A natural man hath no power to receive Christ, as we learn from 1 Corinthians 2:14. The natural man is unwilling to be wrought upon, that he may be made capable to receive the grace of God."[23] "While life is continued, and the means of grace afforded to a people, that is the season wherein God meaneth to lead the soul to receive life and salvation."[24]

This passage is followed by a most earnest and tender appeal to the hearers to give themselves up at once to the Saviour, who is even now waiting for their acceptance.

In another volume, Hooker says,

Every man in his natural state is fastened and settled in sin and corruption. They are in slavery to sin. But God draws the hearts of sinners, first, by giving them light; then by the manifesting of His mercy, namely, by his readiness to receive sinners, by his calls and entreaties to them to come, by his patience in waiting for them. He also draws them by their own consciences, which warn them of their sin, and bear witness against it. More than all, he draws them by his Spirit.[25]

In "The Saints Dignity and Duty" we read,

Christ gave himself to incarnation that he might be the ransom of the guilty. He suffered the wrath of God. He made a covenant with the Father, and He gave a perfect price, for

---

22 Ibid., 54.
23 Ibid., 85.
24 Ibid., 160.
25 Thomas Hooker, *The Unbeliever's Preparing for Christ* (London: Thomas Cotes, 1638), 44.

the full payment of whatever is due to God for all those for whom He paid it.

Without further quotation, it is but just to say that Hooker sets forth the truth with great spiritual discrimination, great tenderness, and fidelity, and with a sweet reasonableness, which must have commended the Gospel to the people to whom the sermons contained in these volumes were preached.

Samuel Willard and the *Body of Divinity*

We pass over half a century, to the time of President Willard. There had been a decline in the religious spirit of the people during that period. The prevalent Calvinism was stated in harsher and more dogmatic forms. Willard's *Body of Divinity* was begun in the latter part of the seventeenth century. It was the earliest folio on theology published in this country, and the largest book that had been published on any subject.[26] It is in the form of lectures on the Shorter Catechism. It is valuable as a statement, by an able man, of the theological system which had prevailed for half a century before President Edwards set forth his Improvements in theology.

President Willard expounded very clearly the external and internal evidence of the divine authority of the Bible. He taught the doctrine of verbal inspiration. The justice of God, he says, is His "inclination to render to all their due according to rule."[27] The benignity of God is "God willing bountifully to bestow the good things of this life upon sinners."[28] "Election is an act of grace. Redemption is an act of pure grace." Election is absolute, not hypothetical. The subjects of election

---

26 Samuel Willard, *A Complete Body of Divinity* (Boston: B. Green and S. Kneeland, 1726), 917 pages.

27 Ibid., 75.

28 Ibid., 84.

are a definite number of men. "There are some men to whom God doth not afford the means and offices of Salvation, and they must needs perish." "Adam stood not as a private, but a public person. He was the representative, and the common stock of all mankind. All men were in him. If they were in him, and sinned in him, how can they be other than sinners? Adam sinned and all sinned in him."[29]

"God is under no obligation to redeem men before His good pleasure."[30] "God's love of certain persons is not the cause of their election, nor is His hatred of others the cause of their reprobation." "The last end of God's election is the manifestation and exaltation of the glory of His grace." "Reprobation is the predestination of a definite number of men for the manifestation of the glory of God's revenging justice in them."[31] But "reprobation doth not take away the liberty of the creature. God made no man on purpose to damn him."

He gives abundant space to the subject of Redemption. The humanity of Christ, he says, "was a complete undivided human nature." "The body of Christ had its natural origin from his mother."[32] The satisfaction by which Christ made reconciliation was given to the justice of God. He suffered the penalty for our sin. Christ died for the elect. "The covenant of redemption must last as long as there are any of God's elect to be born." "Christ died for a select company that was known to him, by name, from eternity."[33]

"In his natural state, no man hath any seed of faith in him. His only capacity is a capacity to receive faith." "The cause of effectual calling is the everlasting love of God." The Spirit of God deals with the understanding and the will. He changes the will. The ability is from

---

29 Ibid., 196-197.
30 Ibid., 251.
31 Ibid., 266-269.
32 Ibid., 297-300.
33 Ibid., 383-384.

God. We are persuaded and enabled to embrace Christ. The terms are presented, and the sinner is made willing.[34] "There is a miserable impotency and malignity of will with respect to holy choices." The will remains a will, however. It has not lost its natural power. It cannot be forced. But a divine change is necessary. The new principle of saving grace in the will and the affections is from God. "We are passive in conversion," and yet "there is an active as well as a passive conversion." "The man is dead. When the Spirit has given him life, then he is active in conversion." "Justification is immutable: therefore a justified person can never again come under a Law-guilt." "In sanctification there is a new power or ability put into the man." "A natural man can contribute nothing to his own conversion."[35]

These quotations are perhaps enough to give a correct impression of this theology of the later Puritan age. The difference between this and the teachings of the earlier divines like Hooker and Norton is that President Willard places the emphasis upon the divine work in our salvation, so as to leave little room for the use of motives addressed to free and responsible beings, while Hooker and Norton are chiefly concerned to develop a sense of responsibility and of obligation. Theirs was a theology that could be preached.

34 Ibid., 428-436.
35 Ibid., 503.

11

THE HALF-WAY COVENANT AND CHURCH MEMBERSHIP

•

THE theological views of our forefathers were influenced by their experiences in their new homes, quite as much as by the writings of their divines. If some of their opinions were severe, there was, after all, a fountain of gentleness and kindness in the heart of the typical Puritan.

One of the remarkable episodes in New England history relates to the Half-Way Covenant, which was approved by the Synod of 1662, and which was in use for more than a hundred years. The Puritans seem to have adopted this, partly on account of their interest in their children and grandchildren, who were growing up in the Colonies which they had planted in the wilderness. It was the easier for them to make this departure from the method of the first generation of Colonists, because the Puritans were never rigid Separatists. There was a good deal of truth in the remark of Roger Williams, that the "Churches of the Bay Colony were unseparated Churches." Although they followed the pattern of the Church in Plymouth in the organization of their Churches, they still regarded the Church of England as their "Dear Mother;" and they had not forgotten its methods of baptism, and confirmation, and hereditary membership.

The early Puritans had made it a cardinal doctrine that none should be members of the Church except those who gave evidence that they had been regenerated by the Holy Spirit. They believed that the corruptions of the Church of England were due to the easy terms on which persons had been admitted to the Lord's Table. They attempted to limit the membership in their new churches to those who were able to relate an experience of a work of grace in their souls. And yet they desired, in some way, to bring their infant children into some connection with the Church.

"We find in Scripture," they said, "that the Lord is very tender of His grace, that He delighteth to manifest and magnify the riches of it, and that He cannot endure any straining or eclipsing thereof, which is both dishonorable unto God, and injurious unto men. And in special, He is large in the Grace of His Covenant, which He maketh with His visible Church and people, and tender of having the same straitned. Hence, when He takes any into Covenant with Himself, He will not only be their God, but the God of their seed after them in their generations. . . . Hence, we dare not, with the Anti-paedobaptist, exclude the infant children of the faithful from the covenant, or from membership in the visible church, and consequently, not from Baptism, the seal thereof."[1]

And so they held, that the children of believers are included with their parents, and are entitled to all church privileges of which infants are capable. Among these privileges was baptism. They baptized their children, because these children were already members of the Church, by reason of the covenant into which their parents had entered. The older divines — Cotton, Davenport, Hooker, and Richard Mather

---

1 Williston Walker, *The Creeds and Platforms of Congregationalism* (New York: Charles Scribner, 1893), 303. Cotton Mather, *Magnalia Christi Americana Volume 2* (Hartford: Silas Andrus, 1820), 239.

— held, in the earlier years, that none but children of "visible saints" should be baptized. But these baptized children constituted a peculiar class in the Puritan churches. They were members, but not in full Communion. Their membership brought to them certain blessings of the covenant. They were hereditary members, and so under the watch and care of the Church. But they were not permitted to come to the Lord's Table, or to vote in the meetings of the Church until they should profess their assent to the doctrines of the Church, and accept its covenant, and give satisfactory evidence that they were born of the Spirit.

Unfortunately, as we shall presently see, the number of those in the Puritan churches who were in full communion was not large. For some reason, the means of grace were not as fruitful as had been expected. So that, in the second and third generations, there was a large number of parents, who were not in "full communion" with the churches. Most of these parents were accounted as members of the churches, because they had been baptized; but they were not communicants. Should they be permitted to present their children for baptism, on the strength of their half-way membership? According to the earlier practice they were not permitted to do so. But it was found that this practice was leaving the majority of the children without baptism.

This matter was earnestly debated in Massachusetts and Connecticut for many years. The tide was turning, and some of the older ministers began to relax the strictness of their views. In 1656, the General Court of Massachusetts summoned a council of ministers, who were designated by name, to meet, with such others as any of the "Confederated Colonies" should send, to clear up the question. The Council met in 1657, in Boston, and decided that all members of the Church had the right to present their children for baptism, though some of them had not the right to come to the Lord's Table.

This decision of the Council, or Assembly, was not accepted as decisive. Some of the leading men, like President Chauncy in Massachusetts, and Mr. Davenport in Connecticut, objected to it, as an abandonment of the principle of a converted Church membership. Finally, the General Court of Massachusetts called a proper Synod, composed of all the ministers and the representatives of all the churches in the Colony. This Synod met in Boston, the second Tuesday in March, 1662. It contained about seventy members, one-third of them ministers. The principal question given to them was this: *Who are the subjects of Baptism?*

After some weeks of consideration and debate, the Synod, by a vote of seven to one, decided in favor of the Half-Way Covenant. They held that parents who had been baptized in infancy, who were not scandalous in life, and who had solemnly owned the covenant before the Church, wherein they gave themselves and their children to the Lord, might present their children for baptism. This was called the Half-Way Covenant, because these parents were in covenant with the Church, not as "visible saints," who had been renewed by the Holy Spirit, and who were prepared to come to the Lord's Table, but only as baptized persons who had an intellectual belief in the truth, and who were living moral lives. These parents were in the Church on account of the faith of their parents, at one remove; and their children were in the Church on account of the faith of their grandparents, at two removes.

The decision of the Synod added intensity to the discussions among the people. A multitude of pamphlets followed, in which one can still read the close and earnest discussions of two hundred and thirty years ago. There were Synodists and Anti-synodists. A decided majority of the ministers favored the Half-Way Covenant. A large number of the people never accepted it. Some of the most learned and able ministers warned the people that the new method would open the doors of the churches to the unworthy, and that it would tend to throw into the shade the work of the Spirit in regeneration. The need of a change of heart would not be felt by those who had not only been admitted to membership in the Church, but who had participated in some of its most sacred rites.[2]

President Chauncy, of Harvard, and John Davenport, of New Haven, led the opposition to the new system, while Wilson and Norton and Mather, among the older ministers, and a large number of the younger ministers were its earnest advocates. Cotton Mather tells us that although the pastors generally favored it, yet in many of the churches a number of the brethren were so decided in their opposition that it was not practicable to follow the recommendations of the Synod. The First Church in Boston, as soon as there was a vacancy in the pastorate, called Mr. Davenport to be their minister on account of his opposition to the Half-Way Covenant. This call led to a division of the church, and the formation of what is now the Old South Church.[3] For some years these two churches did not commune with each other. But those who accepted the new methods were the more numerous party, and the tendency was for those who had been opposed to them to fall in with the common practice. A few churches, however, never accepted the laxer method.

As time went on, the Half-Way Covenant was itself modified. In the beginning, only those who had themselves received baptism, were permitted to own the covenant, and to present their children for baptism. In the time of Cotton Mather, any one who was free from scandalous sins, and from open impiety, could be baptized.[4] "Owning

---

2 Ibid., 258-269.
3 Ibid., 266.
4 Cotton Mather, *Ratio Disciplinae Fratrum Nov-Anglorum* (Boston: S. Gerrish, 1726), 80.

the Covenant" was at first a very solemn profession of a purpose to lead a Christian life. Before the close of the century, however, owning the covenant, and presenting the children for baptism, had become mere forms, which were supposed to have a certain efficacy of their own. In fact, the rites and sacraments of the Puritan churches came to be regarded in the earlier years of the eighteenth century as means of salvation. So the grand-children of the early Puritans approached very nearly the practices which their forefathers had condemned in the Church of England.

As the seventeenth century closed, there was a low type of piety in the churches. With this came, on the one side, a hardening of the doctrines which were preached in the pulpits, and on the other side, a departure from those doctrines, and the adoption of what was then called Arminianism. The necessity of a work of the Spirit to renew and sanctify the heart was no longer insisted on. Revivals of religion were few. There was a tendency to preach morality, instead of to insist upon a really spiritual experience. The venerable Stoddard of Northampton published a sermon, in 1707, in which he maintained that "the Lord's Supper is a converting ordinance, and that sanctification is not a necessary qualification to partaking of the Lord's Supper."[5] These views were accepted in many churches. Discipline was much neglected, and immorality was tolerated. The difference between the Church and the world was fast passing away.

It was not until the Great Awakening, in the time of Edwards, and of Whitefield, that the churches came back to the earlier views in regard to the qualifications for membership in the Church. There were a number of churches that refused to hear Whitefield, or to enter into the new religious movement. These churches held to a dry and lifeless orthodoxy, and placed great reliance upon forms and religious

---

5 Joseph Tracy, *The Great Awakening* (Boston: Tappan & Dennet, 1842), 4.

rites. New England Unitarianism, which was developed toward the close of the eighteenth century, and the beginning of the nineteenth, was the result of a departure from the older religious views, which began in the times of the Half-Way Covenant.

The preaching which led to the great revival gave special emphasis to the work of the Holy Spirit in the change which is called conversion. It led to a sharp discrimination between the Church and the world. The Half-Way Covenant was gradually laid aside, and with it the theory of hereditary Church membership. The new method of stating the doctrines of grace, which was set forth by President Edwards, led to a new style of preaching, which gave prominence to the freedom and responsibility of man. This method of preaching prepared the way for the great revivals of religion which marked the close of the last century and the earlier years of the present century. From those revivals have sprung the great missionary movements of the nineteenth century, and the new and more enterprising spirit in the churches of all denominations, in our times.[6]

---

6 Jonathan Edwards, *An Humble Inquiry into the Rules of the Word of God, Concerning the Qualifications Requisite to a Compleat Standing and Full Communion in the Visible Christian Church* (Edinburgh: William Coke, 1790). Mather, *Magnalia Volume 2*, 278-279. Walker, *Creeds and Platforms*, 280-290. Tracy, *Great Awakening*, 1-40.

12

THE REFORMING SYNOD OF 1679
AND THE SAVOY CONFESSION

•

THE discussion of the influence of the Synod of 1662 has led us far beyond the period to which that Synod belonged. But there was another Synod which had an influence upon the religious views of the fathers of New England, which should have a place in this section.

This was the Reforming Synod of 1679, which met in Boston, September 10th, of that year, at the call of the General Court. It was made up of the Elders and Messengers of the churches of the Colony. It was called to consider two questions: first, "What are the evils that have provoked the Lord to bring His judgments upon New England?" And second, "What is to be done so that these evils may be reformed?"

The people had been suffering from the great Indian wars, and from extensive conflagrations, from shipwrecks, and from the pestilence. They believed that these disasters had come in God's providence, in consequence of their sins; and they set themselves to inquire, with fasting and prayer, for the causes of these great disasters. After mature deliberation the Synod prepared a statement of the evils that were common in the Colony, and presented it to the General Court. This careful official document is preserved in Mather's *Magnalia*, and in other works; and it casts a flood of light upon the religious condition of Massachusetts at the end of the first half-century. I quote only the leading statements, each of which is supported, in the original paper, by a number of particulars. They say,[1]

• There has been a great and visible decay of the power of Godliness amongst many Professors in these churches: communion with God, in His ways of worship, especially in secret, is much neglected.

• The sins of pride, of contention, and of extravagance, abound.

• Servants and the poorer sort of people are guilty in this matter, they go above their estates and degrees.

• Church fellowship is greatly neglected; the rising generation are not mindful of that which their Baptism doth engage them unto.

• Profanity abounds.

• There is much irreverent behavior in the solemn worship of God.

• There is also, much Sabbath breaking.

• Traveling on the Lord's-day is common.

• Family worship is much neglected; the Scriptures are not daily read, that so the word of Christ might dwell richly with them.

• Law-suits are common, brother going to law with brother.

• There is much intemperance. That shameful iniquity of sinful drinking is become too general a Provocation. Days of Training, and other public Solemnities have been much abused in this respect.

• Indians have been debauched, by those who call themselves Christians, who have put their bottles to them and made them drunk also. Instead of converting the Heathen these people have taught them wickedness which before they were not guilty of.

• Church members frequent public Houses and there misspend

---

1 Cotton Mather, *Magnalia Christi Americana Volume 2* (Hartford: Silas Andrus, 1820), 273-278. Williston Walker, *The Creeds and Platforms of Congregationalism* (New York: Charles Scribner, 1893), 426-432.

precious time, unto the dishonor of the Gospel.

• These are heinous breaches of the Seventh Commandment. Temptations thereto are become too common.

• There is unlawful gaming, and an abundance of Idleness.

• There are mixed Dancings; immodest apparel is put on; there is a want of truth amongst men: promise breaking is a common sin, for which New England doth stand ill abroad in the world.

• There is also an Inordinate affection to the world.

• Farms and merchandisings have been preferred before the things of God.

• Religion is made subordinate unto worldly interests.

• Some traders sell their goods at excessive Rates.

• Men are under the prevailing power of a worldly spirit.

• There hath been much opposition to the work of Reformation.

• Sin and sinners have many Advocates.

• A public spirit is greatly wanting in the most of men.

• All seek their own; not the things of Jesus Christ.

• Hence, schools of learning, and other public concerns are in a languishing state, Christ is not prized and embraced in all his offices and ordinances as ought to be.

• Last of all, there is great unfruitfulness under the means of grace.

After these statements of the sins which were most common in New England at that time, the Synod made an earnest appeal to the good people to seek to bring about a reformation. They urged those in official positions, first of all to take the lead in a reform of manners. They advised that none be admitted to the "Lord's Supper without making a personal and public profession of their Faith and Repentance, either orally, or in some other way, — to the satisfaction of the Church." They also urged the duty of attending to discipline in the churches; of seeking to "provide a full supply of officers in the churches;" of providing "for the maintenance of ministers;" of "due care and faithfulness with respect unto the establishment and execution of wholesome laws; especially laws to regulate Public Houses, — to regulate the sale of strong drink; and to punish vice and crime."

They also recommended solemn and explicit renewal of the Covenant in the churches, the confession of sin, and a turning unto the ways of the Lord. The people should "cry mightily unto God, that He would be pleased to rain down Righteousness" upon them.

This appeal of the Synod was heartily seconded by the General Court. The laws against intemperance, and Sabbath breaking, and various forms of vice were more strictly enforced. The churches entered into the work of reformation with great earnestness. Days of fasting and prayer were appointed; there was a solemn renewing of the covenant in many places; the ministers preached frequently, not only on the Lord's-days, but on week days; and, Cotton Mather tells us : "Many thousands will testify that they never saw the special presence of God more notably discovered, than in the solemnities of those opportunities."[2]

The same Synod met again, by adjournment, May 12, 1680, to propose a Confession of Faith. The Boston Synod of 1648 had expressed a hearty assent to the Westminster Confession, "for the substance thereof." But the Congregationalists of England determined to have a Confession of their own. Accordingly, a council, or Synod, met at the Savoy, in London, September 29, 1658, composed of representatives of one hundred and twenty churches. The number of members was about two hundred. The session lasted two weeks. The Synod amended the Confession of the Westminster Assembly in a number of respects, without changing, however, its strong Calvinistic

---

2 Mather, *Magnalia Volume 2*, 283.

statements; and then adopted the amended Confession unanimously, October 12, 1658. The phraseology was improved in a number of sections. A new chapter was added concerning "the Gospel, and the extent of the Grace thereof," which is intensely Calvinistic. In chapter twenty-four, they asserted the principle of toleration in minor matters, for those who do not disturb others in their way of worship. They omitted such parts of the older Confession as set forth the Presbyterian form of Church government; and they added thirty sections relating to Church order, according to the Congregational way.

When the Boston Synod came together, in 1680, for its second session, it proceeded at once to act upon the report of a committee, chosen at its first session, to draw up a Confession of Faith. This committee recommended the adoption of the Savoy Confession, with slight and unimportant amendments. The Synod went carefully through the Confession, adopted the amendments proposed, and then adopted the Confession. The General Court, the next month, approved of this action of the Synod, and ordered that the Confession, with the Platform of 1648, "be printed for the benefit of these churches in present, and after times."[3]

This Confession continued to be the standard of the Congregational churches for almost two hundred years. The National Council of 1865 — which represented not merely the churches of the Colony of Massachusetts, but the Congregational churches of the United States — declared that it embodied substantially the faith of those churches.[4] There have been a number of periods since 1680, when the Congregational churches have taken up certain improvements

---

3 Nathaniel Bradstreet Shurtleff, *Records of the Governor and Company of the Massachusetts Bay in New England Volume 5 1674-1686* (Boston: William White, 1854), 287.

4 James Manning Winchell Yerrinton and Henry Martyn Parkhurst, *Debates and Proceedings of the National Council of Congregational Churches Held at Boston, Mass., June 14-24, 1865* (Boston: American Congregational Association, 1866), 361.

upon the older statements of Calvinism, and the New England the-ology of to-day is much broader than that of the older Confessions; and yet, the Savoy Confession is the only extended and elaborate Confession of Faith which they have ever adopted. The Connecticut Synod, which met at Saybrook, September 9, 1708, also adopted the Savoy Confession, at the same time that they adopted the Saybrook Platform.

13

CALVINISM'S IMPACT ON PURITAN AND AMERICAN SOCIETY

•

IN closing this statement of the religious opinions of the fathers of New England, it is important to point out the influence of this system of religious teaching upon the people.

These doctrines of the older Calvinism were practically the only doctrines that were preached in New England for about a hundred years. They had full sway among a people who were isolated from the great currents of thought in the larger world. In the results of that teaching, we have an indication of what that type of theology is likely to effect. In no other part of the world, except possibly in Scotland, has High Calvinism been given so clear a field in which to develop its full influence.

Positive Benefits of Puritan Calvinism

It should be said, in the first place, that the religious teachings of the early preachers of New England did develop a remarkable type of religious character. We have abundant evidence to show what that type was. There was a high ethical standard, for one thing. The religious men of that time were honest men. Their lives were pure. They brought up their children to fear God, and keep His commandments. They were also devout men. They magnified, above all other things, their personal relations with a personal God, the Father of our Lord Jesus Christ. They believed that they were the elect of God,— the objects of His peculiar care, and destined to an eternal inheritance in heaven. So they lived as pilgrims and strangers on the earth. Their lives were directed by the Providence of God, and they were working out His great plans. No other people have had more reverence for the Bible, or the Sabbath, or the Church, with its ordinances. They were guided by the highest motives. They had the world under their feet. Their training made them good soldiers of Jesus Christ. They had the spirit of the Scottish Covenanters.

Their theological views tended to make them the defenders of liberty. They laid the foundations of the Republic. Their churches were democratic. So were their towns. So were the Colonies, as far as the people were permitted to frame their government. And when George the Third, far on in the eighteenth century, attempted to deprive the English Colonists of their rights as Englishmen, the descendants of these Calvinistic Puritans took the lead in the Revolution which made us a free nation.

Our fathers, also, transmitted to their descendants a vigorous type of manhood, and that type has been perpetuated, among the widely scattered sons of the Puritans, for two centuries and a half. They have been men of convictions, — with the courage of their convictions, — the defenders of liberty, and the champions of the oppressed. It is not too much to claim that this Calvinistic training — like iron in the blood — gave tone and quality to the New England character.

Religious Intensity vs. Extension

So much may be justly claimed for the results of the religious training in the early times in New England. But there were other results of that training which were not so desirable. That which religion gained in *intensity* in those times, it lost in *extension*. The religious teaching and discipline, which made a small number eminent in piety, left the largest part of the people outside the churches.

The first generation of Colonists were a selected class. God had sifted them out from the mass of their countrymen, that they might be the seed for a new Christian nation. They were men of eminent piety. They were devout men. They walked humbly before God. Religious ideas and religious motives guided their plans of life. But it was not so good with the second generation. The majority of the sons of the Puritans never became communicants in their churches. Lechford says, that at the time of his visit, in 1641, only a quarter of the people were members of the churches.[1] As none could become voters in the Colony of Massachusetts who were not communicants, it was a subject of complaint, at all periods of its history, that only a minority of the male adults could have any share in the government. Mr. Palfrey states, as the result of careful investigation, that, in 1670, the number of freemen in Massachusetts was between ten and twelve hundred. That was equal to a quarter or a fifth part of the adult males in the Colony.[2] It is true that some male members of the churches did not become freemen; but the number of such was never large. So that it appears to be true that only about a quarter of the grown men in the Colony were communicants in the churches. This fact was frequently referred to in the political discussions of those times. This large number of disfranchised people complained of the injustice that was done them. From time to time concessions were made to their

---

1 Thomas Lechford, *Plain Dealing or News from New England* (Boston: J.K. Wiggin & W.P. Lunt, 1867).
2 John Gorham Palfrey, *History of New England Volume 3* (Boston: Little Brown, 1858), 41 and *Volume 2*, 8, note.

demands. These facts show very plainly that a large proportion of grown people were outside the churches. These noncommunicants were the children of the Puritans. Very few came into the Colony from Europe after 1642. These were the very persons who, under favorable conditions, would have been most likely to come into the churches. Why was it that the children of the Puritans were not prepared to become members of the churches? There was something pathetic in the complaints which the fathers were continually making of "the great unfruitfulness under the means of grace." We have seen that it was the consciousness of this "unfruitfulness" that led to the Half-Way Covenant. They hoped to prepare their sons and daughters for "full communion," by admitting them to some of the privileges of the Church. But this expedient failed. Those who came into the churches were not benefited, unless there had been a work of God's Spirit in their souls.

If we compare the "fruitfulness under the means of grace," in the first century of our history, with that in the present century, we shall find that we have at present one in five of the people of the United States, a communicant in some one of the Protestant churches. This is, not one in five of the adults, but one in five of all who are counted when the census is taken; persons of all ages, from infancy upwards, including a great many millions of people of foreign birth and training, and with alien languages. But the Puritans had a population of pure English blood, and of Puritan training.

New England Theology

Another very significant fact relating to the Puritan churches in the first century is this: they did not succeed in maintaining a vigorous spiritual life among Christians. There were times when the religious spirit rose very high. But there were also times of long-continued declension, when it seemed to good men that "the glory was departing from New England."

The election sermons preached in Massachusetts in 1668 by Stoughton, 1669 by Thomas Walley, and 1670 by Samuel Danforth, all speak of such a declension at the time of the Reforming Synod. The statement of Thomas Prince is that "a little after 1660 there began to appear a Decay: And this increased to 1670, when it grew very visible and threatening, and was generally complained of and bewailed bitterly by the Pious among them: And yet much more to 1680, when but few of the first generation remained."[3] These statements are confirmed by the Result of the Synod of 1679. The earnest religious services which followed the Reforming Synod were of use in checking the downward tendency, and yet, the religious life in New England between 1680 and 1735 was very far below the expectations of the fathers.

Revivals of religion were few. Dissensions arose in the churches which led, in some instances, to divisions. The fanaticism and cruelty which attended the proceedings relating to witchcraft were partly the result of the decay in the religious life of New England. There was a movement, toward the end of the sixteenth century, in Massachusetts, to strengthen the system of Church government, in the hope that by this means the churches might be protected from false doctrines, and prepared to enforce Church discipline. This movement, which failed in Massachusetts, was successful in Connecticut, and led to the adoption of the Saybrook Platform in 1708.

Still the process of declension went on. The statements which are made in the works of President Edwards, and in the journals of Mr. Whitefield, and the writings of others who had a leading part in the

---

3 "The Decay of Religion in New England," *The Christian History* No. 12, May 21, 1743, 93-96.

Great Awakening show that the condition of the churches was even worse than it had been at the time of the Reforming Synod.[4]

It appears further, from the writings of the younger Edwards, that the High Calvinism which was preached here so long, finally lost its hold upon the people, in consequence of the spread of what was called in those times Arminianism. There is abundant evidence that during the first third of the eighteenth century, a large number of the pastors became Arminians. Dr. Edwards says, "The Calvinists were nearly driven out of the field by the Arminians, Pelagians, and Socinians. The Calvinists appealed to Scripture," he adds, "in support of their peculiar tenets, but the sense in which they interpreted the sacred writings was inconsistent with human liberty, moral agency, accountableness, praise, and blame. It was inconsistent with all command and exhortation, with all reward and punishment. The Calvinists themselves began to be ashamed of their own cause, and to give it up, so far at least, as it relates to liberty and necessity."[5]

"But Mr. Edwards," he continues, "put an end to this seeming triumph of theirs." He points out the "Improvements in Theology" which his father had introduced, such as "the difference between natural and moral necessity, and inability;" the nature of true holiness; the origin of evil; the doctrine of Atonement; of imputation; and of regeneration. President Edwards "proved that the Atonement does not consist in the payment of a debt," but that the suffering of Christ establishes "the authority of the divine law," and "supports the divine government," so that "God without the prostration of His authority and government

---

4 Sereno Edwards Dwight, *The Life of President Edwards* (New York: G. & C. & H. Carvill, 1830), 120. See also George Whitefield, *The First Two parts of His Life with His Journals* (London: W. Strahan, 1756), and Robert Philip, *The Life and Times of George Whitefield* (London: J. R. and C. Childs, 1838) and Joseph Tracy, *The Great Awakening* (Boston: Tappan & Dennet, 1842).

5 Tryon Edwards, *The Works of Jonathan Edwards Volume 1* (Andover: Allen, Morrill & Wardwell, 1842), 481-482.

can pardon and save those who believe."

It is quite possible that some of these strong statements need to be modified. The estimate of the older theology which Dr. Edwards sets forth was doubtless influenced by his own decided leanings toward the new divinity which the elder Edwards had done so much to recommend. But after making all necessary allowances for the personal element in his statements, the evidence is conclusive that the extreme High Calvinism of the earlier Puritan divines had proved insufficient to meet the needs of the later generations of New England people, and that, too, under the most favorable conditions of which we can readily conceive. It failed to do justice to the great truths concerning the Love of God, in the Work of Redemption, and in the free offers of salvation. It also failed to present the claims of God so as to develop the sense of responsibility, which commends the call of God to every man's conscience.

The elder Edwards — our greatest theologian thus far — was enabled to relieve that system of some of its difficulties, so as to give to Consistent Calvinism a new lease of life. Out of these Improvements in Theology there grew a new method of preaching. The great revivals of 1730 to 1750 were the results of this new method of presenting the truth to men. Since the Edwardean period, there has been in the Puritan churches of New England a modified Calvinism, which has been called the New England Theology.

The successors of Edwards — Hopkins, Smalley, the younger Edwards, Emmons, and the others — have followed out his principles along two divergent lines. So that, whatever else may be said of those theological views which have prevailed in New England for the last century and a half, it cannot be said that they have been entirely borrowed from others, or that they have been received without original and thorough examination. It is safe to predict that the theology of the future, among the Puritan churches of New England, will be developed along the lines which were marked out by President Edwards.

14

RELIGIOUS LIFE IN EIGHTEENTH CENTURY NORTHERN NEW ENGLAND: THE EXAMPLE OF THE CHURCH IN BRUNSWICK

•

An Address at the Hundred and Fiftieth Anniversary of the
Congregational Church in Brunswick

AT the close of the seventeenth century, less than half of what is now called New England had been settled. There were a few strong towns in New Hampshire, and a few settlements on the coast of Maine. As the people of Puritan descent pushed their way northward, to settle and cultivate what is now Maine, New Hampshire, and Vermont, they organized their towns and their churches according to the Puritan models. Those new communities passed through experiences not very different from those through which the people in southern New England had passed a hundred years earlier. It was, in many respects, the Puritan history over again.

Yet there were decided differences between the older and the newer churches. Many of the most perplexing questions had been settled during the first generation. There was a well-defined polity for the churches. The system of administration had been slowly learned from experiences in the town and the county and the Province. The new churches were likely to receive encouragement and material aid from the older and stronger churches. Southern New England did a great deal of Home Missionary work in northern New England, long before the west was opened for such work. There was a greater diversity of race and nationality when the later churches were gathered. In many of the newer towns the Scotch Presbyterians were as numerous as the descendants of the Puritans. It took a generation or two for these elements to harmonize. The war of the Revolution affected these newer settlements more than it did those that were older, because they were more exposed to attacks from the Indians, and from the English in Canada.

It is worthwhile, therefore, to study the religious life in northern New England in the eighteenth century. To do this, let us take a representative church in Maine, in the town of Brunswick, which was settled in the early years of the century. The first settlers began very early to make provision for the preaching of the Gospel. Sometimes at Fort George, sometimes in private dwellings, or in barns, and later in the first meeting-houses, — for there were two, on opposite sides of the township, — they came together to worship God. It is plain, from such records as have come down to us, that the early settlers cared a good deal for these religious services.

Among the reasons which the inhabitants of Brunswick urged, in their petition for a charter, in 1735, were these: "That a commodious meeting house has been erected, and a pious and orthodox minister secured," and that they desired to be vested with power to tax themselves for his maintenance. This commodious meeting-house was located midway between the old Fort and Maquoit. The *History* of the town contains a picture of this meeting-house.

It was a plain building, facing the south, with a projecting porch, but without a tower or steeple. The records do not give the dimensions of the edifice, but they give glimpses of its interior. The walls were unfinished; there was no ceiling; the roof timbers were in view; there was a high pulpit, with a sounding-board above it. There was a gallery, and both the gallery and the floor of the church had pews, large and square; and each pew had seats on three sides. The environment of this "commodious meeting-house" was characteristic of the times. In front stood the stocks; in the rear was the whipping-post; nearby was the graveyard. North of the graveyard was a pound, with a substantial fence, and a gate securely locked. Within the house, far up under the roof, was a loft used as a powder magazine.[1]

This was the place of worship for the people of the west side of Brunswick for about seventy years, until after Bowdoin College was founded. In that pulpit Robert Rutherford preached seven years, and Robert Dunlap thirteen years, up to 1760. Those were times of great peril to the pioneers, when block houses were built for defense against the Indians. It is related that when Mr. Dunlap went to Newmeadows to preach, he was escorted by his neighbors, who went armed to the place of prayer. In that pulpit also, John Miller preached twenty-four years, which included the period of the Revolutionary War, and Ebenezer Coffin eight years. These together cover fifty-two years of somewhat regular pastoral work in the eighteenth century.[2]

These are the outward facts. But underneath all this there must have been a religious spirit and life of which we can gain little knowledge from any records that are now extant. The records of the First Parish relate very naturally to secular matters, such as the arrangements for the settlement and the dismission of pastors, the assessment of the parish taxes, repairs of the meeting-house, and other matters of a business nature. Whenever there was any lack of harmony among the members of the church, it was very apt to leave some trace upon

---

1 George Augustus Wheeler and Henry Warren Wheeler, *History of Brunswick, Topsham and Harpswell Maine* (Boston: Alfred Mudge & Son, 1878), 367.

the records. It may be that such records give undue prominence to these things. But of the spiritual life of the people, — of their religious habits, of the quality of the preaching they were able to get, of the doctrines which they accepted, and of the spiritual power of the Church in the last century, — the records give us less information than they do of the votes passed to determine the location of the meeting-house, or the salary of the minister. We should like to know more than we do of the religious life of the people who lived in those times of simplicity and of comparative poverty. In respect to these matters, the indirect evidence is more abundant than that which is direct.

The Relationship between Town and Church

One thing which affected the religious life in Brunswick was the connection of the Church with the state. It is not quite certain that the church had been organized when Mr. Rutherford became the minister, by vote of the town of Brunswick, or even when Mr. Dunlap began his ministry. The people of the town called the minister by vote in town-meeting. The contract was made between the town and the minister. His salary was raised by a tax, levied upon all the rate-payers. After the church was organized, it had the right, under the laws of Massachusetts, to choose its minister, and the town had the right to accept or reject the candidate whom the church had selected. The laws required that every town should be constantly provided with a minister, and if it should neglect for six months to secure an "able, learned, and orthodox minister, of good conversation," the town was liable to be prosecuted and fined for such neglect. Brunswick was prosecuted and fined in 1810 under that law. It was not always easy for the church and the town to agree in the choice of a minister. In a good many instances the minister who had been chosen by the church was rejected by the town. In 1786, the town voted to dismiss the pastor, but the church voted to retain him. Whereupon, the town voted not to raise any money for his support.

There was always more or less trouble in collecting the tax levied for the support of the pastor. Twenty-one persons were sent to jail, in a parish not far from Brunswick, because they refused to pay the tax assessed upon them for the support of the minister of the town. We have evidence of this from the records of an address that Mr. Harlow gave at Cape Elizabeth.

The connection of Church and state did not work as well in Maine as it had done in Massachusetts. It was not as easy to continue that connection after the Revolution, as it had been before. The growth of a spirit of personal independence, under a republican government, and the increasing diversity of religious opinions, made it a hard matter for a church and a town to get on with harmony and good feeling in the support of religious institutions. So that the time came, in the natural course of events, when the connection which had existed so long became a hindrance to the prosperity of religion in the town.

Presbyterianism, Congregationalism and Church Government

The difference of opinion in respect to Church government was also a great obstacle to the prosperity of religion in Brunswick. The first church was probably organized as a Presbyterian church, and in its earlier history it was connected with the Presbytery of Londonderry. Mr. Dunlap was a Presbyterian from mature conviction, as well as by his training. The people in the west part of the town were, for the most part, Scotch-Irish Presbyterians, while those at New Meadows were Congregationalists. The Presbyterians were the more decided in their preferences, because that had been the polity of their fathers. The Congregationalists were not disposed to yield, because New England was full of churches of their order, and theirs was, in some sort, the State Church. There were never more than ten Presbyterian churches in Maine at one time, while the Congregational churches in the district greatly outnumbered them. In a small town on the frontier, a hundred years ago, the questions between these denominations seemed more important than they seem to us at this time.

Nevertheless, there was a spirit of conciliation. In 1774, the church in Brunswick voted that the Sacrament of the Lord's Supper should be administered "at the West meeting-house from the long table, the communicants sitting around it, or in the body-pews, as they might see fit;" and that in the East meeting-house it should be according to "the Congregational form." "Baptism was to be in either form, as persons might choose." There was a difference in respect to singing, and, in 1786, the town voted "to allow the people at the East-end to regulate the way of singing in Divine service in the East-end as they shall think proper." The same year, the church voted against the new way of singing adopted at the East-end of the town, and directed that the psalms and hymns should be read by the deacon, line by line.

Some in the church desired to have ruling elders appointed, while others wished to have deacons. The discipline of the church suffered on account of these disagreements, and the relation between pastor and people was sometimes weakened by them. But, as the larger number of those who came to Brunswick from other places were Congregationalists, the Presbyterians gradually lost the control, and, by the end of the century, the church had become to all intents a Congregational church. This tendency was strengthened by the establishment of Bowdoin College.

Humble Beginnings and Growth

Through all this period Brunswick was but a modest and obscure settlement among the pines. On every side except the river, the dwellings stood close up to the forest, which stretched away for miles. The principal business of the place was the trade in lumber.[3] The people commonly went on foot to the church. Some of those who lived at a distance owned a horse, a saddle, and a pillion, which would accommodate a man, his wife, and one or two children. It is a matter of dispute whether there were two or three wheeled chaises in town before the Revolution.

The New England meeting-houses were not warmed in the last century, and those in these northern regions were not lighted. The people who came in from their long walk through the snow were a strong and hardy race, else they could not have endured the cold, as they sat, in this unfinished house, through the long services. The services in those days were held in the daytime.

But through all this period of hardship and poverty the church continued to grow and to prosper. There is reason to believe that public worship was maintained with a good measure of regularity, — that the sacraments of the Church were administered, and that the standard of piety was a high one. We have the names of more than a hundred who were members of the church before the year 1800, and the list is known to be incomplete.

The service of song in the last century was more simple than it is now. The number of tunes used in public worship was very limited, and there was probably no instrumental music in the earlier years. The choirs were large in those days, and the chorister was a person of great importance. In 1763, the church voted to use "the version of the psalms by Tate and Brady, with the hymns of Dr. Watts annexed thereto."

---

3 Nehemiah Cleaveland, *History of Bowdoin College* (Boston: James Ripley Osgood, 1882), I.

Northern New England Ministers and Theology

The ministers of those times had a position in the community very different from that of their successors in this century. They were still settled for life. The towns were required by law to pay their salaries. They were distinguished from other people by their dress and their manners. The description of Rev. Samuel Eaton, minister in Harpswell from 1764 to 1822, by Professor Alpheus S. Packard, is very graphic.

> He was above the average stature, with a large frame, and full habit. His entrance into the church, on the Sabbath, and his stately progress up the broad aisle, — bowing to the sitters on each side, according to the custom of those days, always attracted attention. He wore a broad skirted coat, with wide pocket flaps, a waistcoat flaring in front, and falling to the knees, breeches, high shoes with large plated buckles, — the whole surmounted with a capacious wig and a cocked hat.[4]

Yet those ministers, with all their dignity, and stateliness, had a great deal of human nature about them. They put on their courtly manners, according to the customs of their time, but there was genuine manhood underneath the manners. The pictures of President McKeen which we are accustomed to see, represent him in the dress of his times, with his long hair gathered in a queue. He was the pastor of the church in Beverly, Massachusetts, from 1785 to 1802. He was above the ordinary stature, and of commanding appearance, and dignified manners. In the earlier years of his ministry, he was fond of athletic sports. One day a visitor at his house in Beverly was boasting

---

4 Ibid., 74 and William Buell Sprague, *Annals of the American Pulpit Volume I* (New York: Robert Carter, 1857), 612-613.

of his strength and skill as a wrestler; whereupon the minister invited him to retire to a suitable place that they might both test their abilities in that line. The proposal was accepted, and they went out. But the minister was too much for the athlete and, after repeated falls, he acknowledged that the pastor was the better man.[5]

The use of intoxicating drinks was more common in those days than now. Parson Smith speaks of an ordination at New Gloucester, in 1765, as a "jolly ordination." He says, "We lost sight of decorum." The progress of the ministers toward the practice of total abstinence from strong drink was slow. It was not till 1813 that the Cumberland Association voted that "there be no ardent spirits used by the Association as a body in future."[6] That vote casts a suggestive backlight upon the social customs of our clerical fathers.

What were the religious teachings in the old meeting-houses? We have a good many sources of information. In the latter part of the eighteenth century the opinions that had been held by the older Puritans had been modified, partly through the influence of President Edwards, and the divines of his school, and a more liberal, and, as we think, a more Biblical, theology began to be preached. Mr. Dunlap had been trained in the more rigid Scottish School. He is said to have been vehement, and persuasive in his style of preaching, and to have taken the celebrated Mr. Whitefield, whom he had met soon after his arrival in this country, as his model. But his successor, Mr. Miller, was a decided Congregationalist, and he probably preached the New England theology. He is said to have been very charitable in his treatment of those who differed with him in religious matters. All the ministers of the church in Brunswick during the last century were Calvinists (except possibly, Mr. Coffin), and they gave their people

5 William Buell Sprague, *Annals of the American Pulpit Volume 2* (New York: Robert Carter, 1857), 219.

6 Centennial Pamphlet, Cumberland Association of Congregational Ministers.

the strong meat of the Gospel.

That was before the time of Sunday-schools in New England. The children were taught the catechism at home, and in the day-schools. They were also catechized by their pastors. The Bible was carefully taught to the children, in the last century, by their fathers and mothers; and it is not certain but they had a better knowledge of the Scriptures, and of the religious truths which they teach, than the children of our own times.

Continued Revival and Growth

The methods of pastoral visiting in the last century were more systematic and thorough than those to which we have been accustomed. The ministers were expected to go from house to house, and teach religious truths to the people, especially to the young people. They were also in the habit of conversing with each individual in regard to his religious duties, and to use their personal influence to lead them forward in a religious life. Here is a record made by a pastor in Maine of his method of pastoral visiting in 1766, and preserved for us in Greenleaf's *Ecclesiastical Sketches*:

First to salute the house: — compare the lists with the family: and note how many know the catechism, how many have taken the covenant, — and how many are church members. Then, to exhort the young people to give attendance to reading, — to secret prayer, — to public worship, — the observance of the Sabbath, — to live peaceable and faithful lives, — to seek the grace of God, and a true conversion. To address parents about their spiritual state, — secret devotions, — family worship, — government, — catechizing, — public worship, — the sacraments, — if they are church members, see to what profit, — if in error or vice, to reclaim, — if in divisions, heal, — if poor, help, — lastly, pray with them all.[7]

It is not surprising that the pastor who followed that method, relates that after a few months of that sort of work, there was a general revival of religion in the town: "A solemn, sweet, and glorious season," that "many of God's people were filled with the joy of the Lord, and that many were brought to see their need of that Saviour whom they had shamefully neglected, and wickedly crucified." It is not surprising that this work of grace extended into the adjoining towns.

The revivals of religion, during the latter part of the eighteenth century, were very wonderful. I have read of a work of grace in Harpswell, Maine, in 1756, which brought sixty-seven persons into the church, in that small community; of another, in North Yarmouth, in 1791, which pervaded the whole town, and brought one hundred and fifty into the church; of another in New Gloucester, in 1791, which was exceedingly powerful.[8] These revivals were all in the vicinity of Brunswick. It is well known that the last years of the last century, and the earliest years in this, were marked by very thorough and extended revivals of religion in all parts of New England.

The establishment of Bowdoin College at Brunswick has had a great influence upon the church. The first building for the College was erected in 1798. It was ready for use in 1802, at which time a house was erected for the President. The first class was graduated in 1806.

President McKeen (elected 1801) used to preach on Sunday, either in the meeting-house of the First Parish, or in the College chapel. From that time to the present, there has been a close connection

7 Jonathan Greenleaf, *Sketches of the Ecclesiastical History of the State of Maine* (Portsmouth: Harrison Gray, 1821), 133, note.

8 Ibid., 68-70, 64-67, 117-123.

between the College and the church. This connection has given to the church a great increase of influence and of usefulness.

Conclusion

If I were asked to state the essential and permanent qualities in the religious life of New England, during the eighteenth century, I should answer: Today is the child of yesterday, — this century is the child of the last century. New England owes its special characteristics to the Pilgrims and the Puritans. The religious life into which we have entered is a continuation of that of our fathers. They planted the seed, and we are reaping the harvests. If we have made some improvements in theology, so did they. If we have entered into the work of reform, so did they. If we have been favored with revivals of religion, so were they.

Our Bible and Tract Societies, our societies for Home, and Foreign Missions, which grew up in New England in the earlier decades of this century, are the results of their religious training and example. That which we are doing, with our more abundant means, and our more fortunate environment, to make human life sweeter, and purer, and to make the world freer and happier, and to enlarge the kingdom of Christ among men, — much of this is the flowering and fruitage from the planting of our fathers, who in the great straightness of their lives, with much self-denial, and with devout prayer laid the foundations of our free Christian Commonwealths. The Pilgrims and the Puritans did not live in vain. Their influence has gone out into all the earth. We are drinking at the fountains which they opened. We walk in their light, and we are to pass on the torch to other generations.

BIBLIOGRAPHY

•

"The Decay of Religion in New England," *The Christian History* No.
12, May 21, 1743, 93-96.

Adams, Charles Francis. *Three Episodes of Massachusetts History Vol.
1*. Boston and New York: Houghton Mifflin, 1892.

Bradford, William. *History of Plymouth Plantation*. Boston: Little
Brown, 1856.

Campbell, Douglas. *The Puritan in Holland, England, and America*.
New York: Harper & Brothers, 1893.

Centennial Pamphlet, Cumberland Association of Congregational
Ministers.

Clap, Roger. *Memoirs of Roger Clap*. Boston: David Clapp, Jr., 1844.

Cleaveland, Nehemiah. *History of Bowdoin College*. Boston: James
Ripley Osgood, 1882.

Colonial Laws of Massachusetts, 29-68. n.p., n.d.

Dexter, Henry Martyn. *Mourt's Relation or Journal of the Plantation
at Plymouth*. Boston: John Kimball Wiggin, 1865.

Dreuillette, Gabriel. *Narré du voyage faict pour la mission des Abnaquiois et des connaissances tiréz de la Nouvelle Angleterre et des dispositions des magistrats de cette république pour le secours contre les Iroquois, ès années 1648 & 1649.* n.p.

Edwards, Jonathan. *An Humble Inquiry into the Rules of the Word of God, Concerning the Qualifications Requisite to a Compleat Standing and Full Communion in the Visible Christian Church.* Edinburgh: William Coke, 1790.

Edwards, Tryon. *The Works of Jonathan Edwards Vol. 1.* Andover: Allen, Morrill & Wardwell, 1842.

Ellis, George Edward. *The Puritan Age and Rule in the Colony of Massachusetts Bay 1629-1685.* Boston: Houghton Mifflin, 1888.

Felt, Joseph Barlow. *The Ecclesiastical History of New England Vol. 1.* Boston: Congregational Library Association, 1855.

Fisher, George Park. *History of the Christian Church.* London: Hodder and Stoughton, 1890.

Fry, Edward. "Quakers" in *Encyclopedia Britannica 9th Edition Volume 20.* Edinburgh: Adam and Charles Black, 1875.

Galton, Francis. *Hereditary Genius: An Inquiry into Its Laws and Consequences.* London: Macmillan, 1869.

George Augustus Wheeler and Henry Warren Wheeler. *History of Brunswick, Topsham and Harpswell Maine* (Boston: Alfred Mudge & Son, 1878), 367.

Goodwin, John Abbot. *The Pilgrim Republic: An Historical Review of the Colony of New Plymouth.* Boston: Houghton Mifflin, 1899.

Green, John Richard. *History of the English People Vol. 3.* New York: Harper & Brothers, 1879.

Greenleaf, Jonathan. *Sketches of the Ecclesiastical History of the State of Maine*. Portsmouth: Harrison Gray, 1821.

Hawthorne, Nathaniel. *The Scarlet Letter*. Boston: James R. Osgood, 1878.

Hooker, Thomas. *The Soul's Vocation or Effectual Calling to Christ*. n.p. 1638.

Hooker, Thomas. *The Unbeliever's Preparing for Christ*. London: Thomas Cotes, 1638.

Hutchinson, Lucy. *Memoirs of the Life of Colonel Hutchinson*. London: Henry Bohn, 1863.

Jefferson, Thomas. *Notes on the State of Virginia*. Richmond: J.W. Randolph, 1853.

Kidd, Benjamin. *Social Evolution*. New York: Macmillan, 1894.

Lechford, Thomas. *Plain Dealing or News from New England*. Boston: J.K. Wiggin & W.P. Lunt, 1867.

Longfellow, Henry Wadsworth. *The Courtship of Miles Standish and Other Poems*. Boston: Ticknor and Fields, 1859.

Longfellow, Samuel. *The Life of Henry Wadsworth Longfellow Vol. 2*. Boston: Houghton Mifflin, 1893.

Lowell, James Russell. *Among My Books* (Boston: Houghton Mifflin, 1882), 242.

Mather, Cotton. *Magnalia Christi Americana Volume 2*. Hartford: Silas Andrus, 1820.

Mather, Cotton. *Ratio Disciplinae Fratrum Nov-Anglorum*. Boston: S. Gerrish, 1726.

Motley, John Lothrop. *History of the United Netherlands Vol. 4*. London: John Murray, 1876.

New England's First Fruits. London: Henry Overton, 1643.

Norton, John. *The Orthodox Evangelist*. London: John Macock, 1654.

Palfrey, John Gorham. *History of New England*. Vols. 1-3. Boston: Little Brown, 1858-60.

Peters, Samuel. *General History of Connecticut*. New York: D. Appleton, 1877.

Philip, Robert. *The Life and Times of George Whitefield*. London: J. R. and C. Childs, 1838.

Records of the Town of Plymouth Volume 1 - 1636 to 1705. Plymouth: Avery & Doten, 1889.

Robertson, Edmund. "Education" in *Encyclopedia Britannica 9th Edition Volume 7*. Edinburgh: Adam and Charles Black, 1875.

Savage, James and John Winthrop. *The History of New England from 1630 to 1649*. 2 vols. Boston: Phelps and Farnham, and Boston: Thomas B. Wait and Son, 1825-26.

Sereno, Edwards Dwight. *The Life of President Edwards*. New York: G. & C. & H. Carvill, 1830.

Shedd, William Greenough Thayer. *Literary Essays*. New York: Charles Scribner's Sons, 1878.

Shepard, Thomas. *The Works of Thomas Shepard Vol 1*. Boston: Doctrinal Tract and Book Society, 1853.

Shurtleff, Nathaniel Bradstreet. *Records of the Colony of New Plymouth in New England 1633-1640, 1644-1657* and *1650-1660*. Vols. 1, 3-4. Boston: William White, 1854-55.

Shurtleff, Nathaniel Bradstreet. *Records of the Governor and Company of the Massachusetts Bay in New England 1650-1660* and *1674-1686*. Vol. 4 Part 1 and Vol. 5. Boston: William White, 1854.

Sprague, William Buell. *Annals of the American Pulpit*. Vols. 1-2. New York: Robert Carter, 1857.

Stead, William Thomas. "Mr. Gladstone - Part 1: The Too Great Orb of Our Fate," *Review of Reviews Volume 5*, April, 1892, 360.

The Colonial Laws of Massachusetts. City of Boston, 1889.

The New England Historical and Genealogical Register Volume 48 1894. Boston: New England Historic Genealogical Society.

Tracy, Joseph. *The Great Awakening*. Boston: Tappan & Dennet, 1842.

Trumbull, James Hammond. *The True-Blue Laws of Connecticut and New Haven and the False Blue-Laws Invented by the Rev. Samuel Peters*. Hartford: American Publishing Company, 1876.

Walker, Williston. *The Creeds and Platforms of Congregationalism*. New York: Charles Scribner, 1893.

Ward, Nathaniel. *The Simple Cobler of Aggawam in America*. Boston: James Munroe, 1843.

Whitefield, George. *The First Two parts of His Life with His Journals*. London: W. Strahan, 1756.

Willard, Samuel. *A Complete Body of Divinity*. Boston: B. Green and S. Kneeland, 1726.

Yerrinton, James Manning Winchell and Henry Martyn Parkhurst. *Debates and Proceedings of the National Council of Congregational Churches Held at Boston, Mass., June 14-24, 1865*. Boston: American Congregational Association, 1866.

About The Greater Heritage

Mission
The Greater Heritage is a Christian publishing ministry that equips believers for an abundant life of service, personal spiritual growth and character development.

What We Do
The Greater Heritage publishes original articles, books, Bible studies and church resources. All of its books are made entirely in the USA.

Want to publish with us? Inquire at:
The Greater Heritage
1170 Tree Swallow Dr., Suite 309
Winter Springs, Florida 32708
info@thegreaterheritage.com
www.thegreaterheritage.com

Find more books and our latest catalog online at:
www.thegreaterheritage.com/shop

THE
Greater Heritage
Christian Publishing

SPREAD THE WORD - SHARE THIS BOOK

If you enjoyed this book, please consider sharing it with others. There are many ways to share, including...

- Take a photo with the book and post it on your social media page(s).

- Write a review on your blog or on an online store's product page.

- Share a copy with friends and family or buy one as a gift.

- Recommend this book to your circle of influence.

- Follow The Greater Heritage on Twitter: @TGH_Ministries.

- Subscribe to our email list at www.thegreaterheritage.com.

Lightning Source UK Ltd.
Milton Keynes UK
UKHW020341210223
417331UK00007B/177/J